QuickCook

QuickCook
Food for Friends

Recipes by Emma Lewis

Every dish, three ways—you choose!
30 minutes | 20 minutes | 10 minutes

An Hachette UK Company
www.hachette.co.uk

First published in Great Britain in 2013 by Hamlyn,
a division of Octopus Publishing Group Ltd
Endeavour House, 189 Shaftesbury Avenue
London WC2H 8JY
www.octopusbooksusa.com

Distributed in the US by
Hachette Book Group USA
237 Park Avenue
New York NY 10017 USA

Distributed in Canada by
Canadian Manda Group
165 Dufferin Street
Toronto, Ontario, Canada M6K 3H6

ISBN 978-0-600-62672-5

Printed and bound in China

10 9 8 7 6 5 4 3 2 1

Standard level spoon and cup measurements are used in all recipes.

Ovens should be preheated to the specified temperature. If using a convection oven,
follow the manufacturer's instructions for adjusting the time and temperature.
Broilers should also be preheated.

This book includes dishes made with nuts and nut derivatives. It is advisable for
those with known allergic reactions to nuts and nut derivatives and those who may
be potentially vulnerable to these allergies, such as pregnant and nursing mothers,
people with weakened immune systems, the elderly, babies, and children, to avoid
dishes made with nuts and nut oils.

It is also prudent to check the labels of prepared ingredients for the possible inclusion
of nut derivatives.

The U.S. Food and Drug Administration advises that eggs should not be consumed
raw. This book contains some dishes made with raw or lightly cooked eggs. It is
prudent for more vulnerable people, such as pregnant and nursing mothers, people
with weakened immune systems, the elderly, babies, and young children, to avoid
uncooked or lightly cooked dishes made with eggs.

Contents

Introduction

30 20 10—Quick, Quicker, Quickest

This book offers a new and flexible approach to planning meals for busy cooks and lets you choose the recipe option that best fits the time you have available. Inside you will find 360 dishes that will inspire you and motivate you to get cooking every day of the year. All the recipes take a maximum of 30 minutes to cook. Some take as little as 20 minutes and, amazingly, many take only 10 minutes. With a little preparation, you can easily try out one new recipe from this book each night, and slowly you will build a wide and exciting portfolio of recipes to suit your needs.

How Does it Work?

Every recipe in the QuickCook series can be cooked one of three ways—a 30-minute version, a 20-minute version, or a superquick and easy 10-minute version. At the beginning of each chapter you'll find recipes listed by time. Choose a dish based on how much time you have and turn to that page.

You'll find the main recipe in the middle of the page with a beautiful photograph and two time variations below.

If you enjoy the dish, you can go back and cook the other time options. If you liked the 20-minute Cod Fillets with Tomatoes and Salsa Verde (see pages 160–161), but only have 10 minutes to spare, then you'll find a way to cook it using quick ingredients or clever shortcuts.

If you really enjoyed the ingredients and flavors of the 10-minute Iced Berries with White Chocolate Sauce (see pages 240–241), why not try the 20-minute White Chocolate Berry Mousses, or be inspired to cook a more elaborate sweet treat using similar ingredients, such as the 30-minute White Chocolate and Berry Cookies. Alternatively, browse through all the 360 recipes, find something that catches your eye, and then cook the version that fits your time frame.

Or, for easy inspiration, turn to the gallery on pages 12–19 to get an instant overview by themes, such as Special Occasions and Party Treats.

QuickCook Online

To make life even easier, you can use the special code on each recipe page to e-mail yourself a recipe card for printing, or e-mail a text-only shopping list to your phone. Go to www.hamlynquickcook.com and enter the recipe code at the bottom of each page.

 FOO-PUDD-DUI

QuickCook Food for Friends

Inviting friends and family over for a bite to eat should be the easiest, most enjoyable thing in the world, but too often most of your time is spent slaving in the kitchen instead of having fun and enjoying dinner together. However, it's easy to produce delicious inspiring dishes in less than 30 minutes, and some are so simple they can be on the table in just 10 minutes—which gives you more time to get on with the important things in life.

Get Ahead

A little planning ahead is always useful when having friends over. Once you've decided on a guest list, you need to organize a menu. Try to think of your guests' taste—find out if you need to cater for any special diets or if there is something people especially love to eat—and then decide on your main dish. Once you've worked this out, it's easier to decide what else to serve. Don't vary cooking styles too much: if you've decided on an Asian-influenced main dish, try to work some of these flavors into the appetizer and dessert, too.

Think about timings when planning what you eat. For a larger meal, it's useful to write down a time plan of when things need to be started. However, no matter the scale of your event, it's always best to cook a few delicious dishes instead of stress out trying to organize a large array of mediocre ones. It's a good idea to focus your effort on one dish, so if you choose a complicated appetizer, keep the main dish simple, with something like pasta. If you choose a show-stopping dessert and main dish, make the appetizer a simple, no-cook salad.

When planning your menu, consider the dish washing. You don't want to be cleaning up the kitchen for hours after your guests have left, so wash up as you go along. If time is really short, cook a one-dish meal; an attractive baking dish or pan that can be taken straight from the stove or oven to the table is a great investment and makes for a relaxing meal.

Set the Scene

To welcome your guests, make sure your home looks its best. A quick cleanup before everyone arrives is essential. Decide where you want to eat: maybe the kitchen for a casual dinner, the dining room for a more formal occasion, or perhaps a buffet table if you have a lot of people coming. A vase of flowers is a quick and easy way of making any room look special. Buy inexpensive seasonal flowers to keep down costs, and if you're planning to put them on the table, make sure they are low enough not to block guests' views of each other.

A beautiful tablecloth will make any meal feel more festive; an antique linen sheet makes an attractive tablecloth. Set the table with plain white china, or mix and match secondhand plates for a cheap and easy retro look. If you're feeling creative, leaves, shells, and ribbons can look effective scattered on the table or arranged around the place settings, while fruits and vegetables can make a decorative centerpiece. Keep the lights in the room low for an inviting, intimate feel— you can, for example, place tea lights around the room or on the table—but make sure it's not so dark that people can't see what they are eating. Finally, decide on what kind music you want to play to set the mood or get the party going. Just make sure the music is low enough for people to carry on conversations.

Stress-Free Cooking

Appetizers

A sit-down appetizer sets the scene for a formal evening— perhaps a birthday dinner or when you want to impress the parents-in-law—and this book includes a tempting range of simple appetizer recipes. On other occasions, it is perfectly acceptable to abandon formal appetizers and set out a selection of nuts, olives, and good-quality chips, served with a cocktail or glass of bubbly. You could provide more substantial nibbles, to which guests can help themselves, such as hams and salami, sun-dried tomatoes, Crispy Tostados (see page 52), Red Pepper Dip (see page 64), Fig and Cheese Crostini (see page 40), or Roasted Eggplant Bruschetta (see page 30).

Main dishes

There are plenty of ways of keeping the main dish simple and quick. A leg or shoulder of lamb will take a while to cook in the oven, but a rack of lamb can be on the table in less than 30 minutes. This makes life easy, but remember that with these leaner, quick-cooking cuts of meat, it really is worthwhile spending extra to get the best quality—you will taste the difference. Fish and seafood are perfect for the host in a hurry because they take so little time to cook and need little more than a squeeze of lemon juice and a simple side dish to turn them into a delicious dinner-party treat. Just remember to shop for them on the day you are planning to cook them, because fresh fish really does taste better.

Vegetarians can sometimes feel cheated at dinner parties, so to make a meal really special, look out for seasonal ingredients— the first asparagus of the season or a perfectly ripe bunch of tomatoes make a great starting point for a meat-free meal. More unusual heritage vegetables or baby vegetables, which are now widely available, are also a wonderful way of perking up a plate and making it look worthy of a restaurant.

The flavor of good-quality basic ingredients will always shine through, and all it takes to enhance them is a little fresh pesto, a drizzle of special oil or vinegar, or a sprinkling of herbs. Keep side dishes simple and fast: a selection of leaves dressed with something special, or maybe some couscous or polenta, which can be ready in 5 minutes flat. Make the most of canned beans, which can be easily blended to make a quick side or appetizer or you can toss them with some dressing and tomatoes to make a hearty salad.

Another way to make the meal a little more special is to use an unusual ingredient. Supermarkets are increasingly catering for our more exotic tastes, and an exciting ingredient can make a meal really memorable. Look out for jewel-like pomegranate seeds, which look pretty on the plate and are great to sprinkle over salads or Middle Eastern dishes. For an Asian dish, try to get some authentic ingredients, such as lime leaves and lemon grass, which will lend your dish a wonderful subtle and different flavor, or go to the trouble of tracking down an authentic curry paste. If you're making a simple Italian supper, search out a different type of pasta than you usually use—perhaps try thick tubelike bucatini or use black squid-ink pasta for a seafood dish. Sometimes it is worth spending a little extra on a key ingredient that can be used sparingly. Creamy rich buffalo mozzarella is a world apart from the regular cow milk version, while just a hint of perfumed saffron will transform a paella. It's also worth remembering that a splash of alcohol really helps to lift a dish—brandy or wine for a classic French dish, a drop vermouth for fish, or try something more unusual, such as sherry, for a Spanish feel.

Desserts
To round off the meal in style, you'll want to prepare something memorable, but this doesn't have to be complicated. Browse through the dessert recipes for inspiration, choosing a 10-minute recipe if you are short on time. Many of the quicker recipes are elegant enough to serve at a formal dinner, including Chocolate Soufflé Wraps (see page 234), Iced Berries with White Chocolate Sauce (see page 240), Lemon Baskets (see page 256), and Warm Mango and Raspberry Gratin (see page 274). For a really stress-free evening, serve a selection of great cheeses with some walnuts and perhaps a bottle of sweet wine, or a colorful bowl of exotic fruit salad.

What to Do If Disaster Strikes
Even the best, most experienced cook will have nights when things go wrong in the kitchen. The most important thing is not to panic; a relaxed, welcoming host is what makes the evening. And the chances are that no one will notice anyway— a name change is often all that is needed. Your defrosted ice cream becomes a mousse, overcooked potatoes turn into instant mashed potatoes and burned onions are passed off as a caramelized onion sauce.

If in doubt, keep some cooked shrimp and a container of good-quality vanilla ice cream on hand in the freezer and a bottle of bubbly in the refrigerator. Popping open the bubbly will keep your guests happy while you whip up a superquick and delicious emergency dinner of shrimp with pasta or a risotto followed by ice cream in next to no time.

Italian Favorites

Everyone loves Italian food, making it a great choice for a dinner party

Clam Pasta with Tomatoes 54

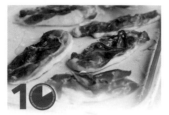

Chicken Saltimbocca 86

Porcini Meatballs 118

Italian Fish Stew 142

Charred Tuna with Peperonata
154

Prosciutto-Wrapped Scallops with Red Peppers and Beans 168

Butternut Risotto with Chile and Ricotta 190

Puttanesca Pizza 210

Eggplant, Tomato, and Mozzarella Melts 222

Vanilla Baked Apricots with Ricotta Cream 236

Coffee Cocktail with Almond Cookies 238

Raspberry Tiramisu 260

Spicy Favorites

Recipes to help you make the most of your spice rack

Chicken and Chermoula Pilaf 82

Spicy Stir-Fried Chicken 84

Pork and Pineapple Curry 100

Rack of Lamb with Harissa Dressing 106

Beef Strips with Tomatoes, Paprika, and Onion 122

Seared Monkfish with Spiced Beans 136

Tomato and Feta Pilaf with Shrimp 138

Tandoori Salmon with Yogurt Sauce 140

Spicy Shrimp and Coconut Curry 152

Spicy Tofu and Mushroom Stir-Fry 186

Spicy Grilled Zucchini with Mashed Chickpeas 218

Cinnamon Plum Crisp 244

Light & Healthy

These fresh, tasty dishes are perfect for a light lunch

Celeriac Remoulade with Ham 38

Asparagus Mimosa 44

Crab and Mango Salad with Chile Lime Dressing 48

Caesar Salad 60

Smoked Duck, Orange, and Watercress Salad 88

Broiled Lamb with Minted Peas 104

Broiled Swordfish with Warm Romesco Salad 132

Thai-Style Squid Salad 156

Tea-Smoked Salmon 166

Sesame-Crusted Tuna with Ginger Dressing 170

Sweet Potato Laksa 196

Miso Eggplant with Cucumber Rice Noodles 202

Hearty & Substantial

Wholesome food to make your guests feel welcome

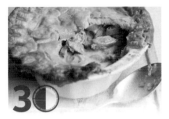

Chicken, Leek, and
Tarragon Pie 78

Herbed Pork with Creamy
Applesauce 98

Seared Beef Fillet with
Horseradish Sauce 120

Manhattan Clam
Chowder 134

Two-Bean Chili with Avocado
Salsa 194

Pepper and Artichoke
Paella 198

Puffed Goat Cheese and
Red Pepper Omelets 206

Carrot and Beet Tabbouleh
212

Mushroom Risotto with
Gremolata 220

Molten Chocolate Cakes 234

Warm Almond Cakes with Fig
Compote 242

Orange and Cinnamon
Puddings with Syrup 276

Special Occasions

Rise to the occasion with the very best ingredients

Crispy Bacon Oysters 42

Whole Baked Brie with Pecans and Maple Syrup 50

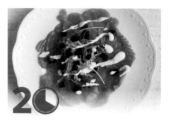

Salmon Carpaccio with Beet Topping 56

Saffron Roasted Chicken 80

Baked Lamb and Red Peppers with Mint Salsa 110

Individual Beef Wellingtons 112

Sea Bream in a Salt Fennel Crust with Lemon Dressing 130

Grilled Lobster with Herb Butter 174

Baked Tomato and Spinach Puffs 180

Strawberry Meringue Roulade 232

Banana Pecan Strudels 254

Warm Chocolate Cherry Tarts 270

Party Treats

Bite-size snacks and food designed for sharing

Bloody Mary Gazpacho 26

Baked Mushrooms with Taleggio and Pesto 34

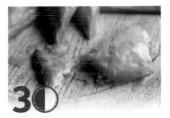

Three Cheese Phyllo Bites 40

Chicken Liver Pâté 68

Vietnamese Beef Skewers 114

Crab and Corn Cakes with Red Pepper Mayonnaise 144

Smoked Haddock and Spinach Tart 150

Citrus-Roasted Salmon 172

Leek and Blue Cheese Tart 204

Chocolate Peanut Butter Whoopie Pies 250

Strawberry Rhubarb Shortcake Slices 266

Honey Ricotta Fritters with Pistachios 278

Relaxed and Informal

Easy-going dishes for a kitchen-table supper

Spanish Shrimp with Chorizo 36

Turkish Pizza with Spinach, Pomegranate, and Feta 46

Crispy Tostados with Avocado and Tomatoes 52

Red Pepper Dip with Herb Pita Crackers 64

Roasted Chicken Breasts with Herb Butter 76

Mustard Rarebit-Style Pork Chops 90

Lamb Steaks with Tomatoes, Feta, and Mashed Chickpeas 108

Grilled Rib-Eye Steak 116

Chickpea Falafel Wraps 188

Date Cakes with Caramel Sauce 246

Individual Pear Crisp with an Oaty Topping 252

Caramelized Custard Tarts 268

Someone to Impress

Delicious show-stoppers worthy of your best china

Squid with Lemon and Capers 32

Blue Cheese Soufflé with Apple and Arugula 58

Thai Pork with Mango Salsa 94

Seared Shrimp with Squid Ink Pasta 128

Hot-Smoked Salmon and Watercress Pasta 146

Roasted Hake with Tomatoes and Pistou 148

Salmon, Dill, and Rice Packages 162

Baked Sea Bass with Tomatoes, Olives, and Oregano 164

Chargrilled Chese with Roasted Olives and Salad 208

Lemon Puddings 256

White Chocolate Rice Pudding Brûlée 262

Passionfruit Cheesecakes 272

QuickCook
Appetizers

Recipes listed by cooking time

30

20

Baked Figs Wrapped in Prosciutto

Serves 4

8 figs
½ cup mozzarella cheese,
   cut into 8 slices
8 slices of prosciutto
½ cup olive oil
2 tablespoons balsamic vinegar
4 cups arugula leaves
salt and black pepper

- Cut a deep cross into the top of each fig, nearly to the bottom, then place a piece of mozzarella inside. Wrap a slice of prosciutto around each fig. Brush the prosciutto with a little oil. Transfer to a baking sheet and cook in a preheated oven, at 425°F, for 7–10 minutes or until the ham is crisp and the cheese starts to melt.

- Meanwhile, whisk together the balsamic vinegar with the remaining oil and season well. Toss most of the dressing together with the arugula leaves and arrange on plates. Add the figs and drizzle with a little more of the dressing. Serve immediately.

1 Fig and Ham Country Salad

Halve 8 figs and brush them with a little olive oil. Heat a ridged grill pan until smoking and then cook the cut sides of the figs for 1 minute, until lightly charred. Wrap each half in a slice of prosciutto. Mix 1 tablespoon finely chopped shallot with 1 tablespoon sherry vinegar and 3 tablespoons olive oil. Toss through 5 cups salad greens and serve with the grilled figs with some soft goat cheese crumbled on top.

3 Fig Tatin with Ham

From a sheet of ready-to-bake puff pastry, cut out 4 circles, about 4 inches across. Heat ¼ cup sugar with 2 teaspoons water in a small saucepan. Let the mixture simmer and turn a dark caramel color. Remove the saucepan from the heat and stir in 2 tablespoons red wine vinegar. Pour the mixture into the bottoms of 4 individual metal molds. Slice 8 figs and place them on top. Put the pastry circles on top of the figs and bake in a preheated oven, at 400°F, for 15–20 minutes, until the pastry is golden. Invert the tarts onto plates and top each with some arugula leaves, a slice of prosciutto, and some shaved manchego or parmesan cheese.

Bloody Mary Gazpacho

Serves 4

2 garlic cloves, chopped

2 celery sticks, chopped, plus
  extra to serve

1 tablespoon chopped onion

4 ripe tomatoes

1¼ cups tomato juice

juice of 2 limes

1 teaspoon celery salt

2–3 tablespoons Worcestershire
  sauce

½ cup vodka (optional)

Tabasco sauce, to taste

lime wedges, to serve

- Put all the ingredients, except the vodka and Tabasco sauce, in a food processor and blend until smooth. Press the mixture through a fine strainer.

- Add the vodka, if using, and Tabasco sauce to taste and pour into glasses. Serve with sprigs of celery and lime wedges.

2. Pita Chips with Gazpacho Salsa

Cut 4 pita breads into thick strips. Toss them together with 2 tablespoons olive oil, spread them out on a baking sheet, and cook in a preheated oven, at 375°F, for 7–10 minutes, until golden and crisp. Let cool. Meanwhile, finely chop 4 tomatoes, ¼ cucumber, and ½ red bell pepper and toss together with 2 crushed garlic cloves, 1 tablespoon sherry vinegar, and 3 tablespoons extra virgin olive oil. Serve the salsa with the pita crisps.

3. Roasted Tomato Gazpacho

Toss 4 halved tomatoes with 3 tablespoons olive oil. Place in a roasting pan with 2 garlic cloves and cook in a preheated oven, at 400°F, for 20 minutes or until soft and lightly browned. Place in a blender with 1 roasted red bell pepper, 2 teaspoons sherry vinegar, 1 crustless slice of bread, and 1¼ cups tomato juice and blend until smooth. Rub through a strainer to remove all the pulp, then season and add a little Tabasco sauce to taste. Chill in the freezer for 5 minutes, then ladle into serving bowls. Sprinkle with 1 tablespoon chopped red onion mixed together with 1 diced avocado.

Spiced Coconut Squash Soup

Serves 4–6

2 tablespoons oil
1 onion, chopped
2 teaspoons finely chopped
   fresh ginger root
½ teaspoon ground coriander
1 lemon grass stalk
1 strip of orange peel
1 butternut squash, peeled
   and chopped
4 cups vegetable stock
½ cup coconut milk
salt and black pepper

To serve

1 red chile, chopped
fresh cilantro leaves, chopped

- Heat the oil in a large saucepan, add the onion, and cook for 5 minutes, until softened. Add the ginger, ground coriander, lemon grass, orange peel, and squash. Pour in the stock and coconut milk and bring to a boil. Let simmer for 12–15 minutes, until the squash is soft.

- Remove the lemon grass and orange peel and use an immersion blender to blend to a smooth paste. Season to taste and divide between serving bowls. Sprinkle with the chile and fresh cilantro to serve.

Grilled Squash and Coconut Salad

Peel and thinly slice ¼ butternut squash. Toss with 2 tablespoons oil, then season and cook on a ridged grill pan for 2–3 minutes on each side, until charred and soft. Whisk 3 tablespoons lime juice with ¼ cup oil and 1 finely chopped chile. Toss the squash together with 5 cups salad greens, a handful of fresh cilantro, and the dressing. Sprinkle with toasted dry coconut to serve.

Coconut Squash Rice

Heat 2 tablespoons oil in a large saucepan, add 1 chopped onion, and cook for 5 minutes, until softened. Stir in 1 crushed garlic clove and 1 teaspoon finely chopped fresh ginger root, followed by 2 tablespoons Thai red curry paste. Add ½ peeled and chopped butternut squash and cook for a couple of minutes, until well coated. Stir through 1⅔ cups jasmine rice. Pour in 2 cups vegetable stock and ½ cup coconut milk. Bring to a boil and cook for 10 minutes, then reduce the heat and simmer gently for 5 minutes, until the rice and squash are just cooked through. Sprinkle with a handful chopped fresh cilantro leaves before serving.

30 Charred Eggplant and Tomato Quesadillas

Serves 4

1 eggplant, sliced
¼ cup olive oil
1 onion, sliced
1 garlic clove, crushed
pinch of cayenne powder
1 tablespoon tomato paste
6 tomatoes, chopped
4 soft flour tortillas
3 oz soft goat cheese
salt and black pepper

- Toss the eggplant with 2 tablespoons oil and season with salt and black pepper. Heat a ridged grill pan until smoking hot, then cook the eggplant for 3 minutes on each side until charred and soft.

- Heat the remaining oil in a saucepan, add the onion, and cook over low heat for 10 minutes, until soft. Stir in the garlic, followed by the cayenne, tomato paste, and tomatoes. Let cook for 5–10 minutes, until the tomatoes are lightly charred.

- Lay the tortillas on a work surface. Spoon some tomatoes over one half of each tortilla, add some eggplant slices, and crumble some goat cheese over the top. Fold each tortilla in half, transfer to a baking sheet, and place under a hot broiler for 2–3 minutes. Carefully turn over and cook for another 2–3 minutes, until golden and crispy all over. Cut into wedges and serve.

10 Roasted Eggplant Bruschetta Thickly slice 1 ciabatta loaf, rub the cut sides with 2 tablespoons olive oil, then cook under a medium-hot broiler for 2–3 minutes on each side, until golden and crisp. Rub the surface of each toast with a peeled garlic clove. Toss ⅓ (10½ oz) jar chopped roasted eggplant with 4 chopped tomatoes, 1 teaspoon balsamic vinegar, 2 tablespoons olive oil, and a handful of chopped basil. Spoon the mixture over the ciabatta and top with a little soft goat cheese before serving.

20 Charred Eggplant, Tomato, and Goat Cheese Pasta Thickly slice 1 eggplant, toss together with ¼ cup olive oil, and place on a baking sheet. Cook in a preheated oven, at 425°F, for 10 minutes. Add 8 halved cherry tomatoes and cook for another 5 minutes, until lightly charred and soft. Heat a large saucepan of salted water and cook 12 oz penne pasta according to the package directions. Drain and return the pasta to the pan. Stir in 2 teaspoons balsamic vinegar, the eggplant, and tomatoes and any juices. Divide among 4 serving bowls and sprinkle with 2 oz hard goat cheese, grated, and a handful of chopped basil.

Squid with Lemon and Capers

Serves 4–6

1 lb prepared squid
¼ cup all-purpose flour
¼ cup cornstarch
1 tablespoon capers, drained and
 coarsely chopped, plus extra
 whole capers to serve
finely grated rind and juice of
 1 large lemon
⅓ cup mayonnaise
2 garlic cloves, crushed
oil, for frying
salt and black pepper

- Cut the squid pouches in half. Score a crisscross pattern across the inside of the squid with a sharp knife, being careful not to cut all the way through, then cut into bite-size pieces. Mix together the all-purpose flour, cornstarch, chopped capers, and lemon rind on a plate and season well.

- Toss the squid in the flour mixture, making sure it is well coated. Heat a large saucepan one-third full of oil. Test to see if it is hot enough by dropping a small piece of bread into it; it should sizzle and brown after 15 seconds. Cook the squid, in batches, for 2 minutes, until golden and crisp, then set aside on paper towels. Briefly fry the whole capers and set aside on paper towels.

- Stir together the mayonnaise and garlic and add lemon juice to taste. Sprinkle some fried capers over the squid and serve with the mayonnaise for dipping.

Grilled Squid and Citrus Salad

Halve 8 oz baby squid, score the inside as above, and cut into bite-size pieces. Toss the squid with 1 tablespoon olive oil and season well. Cook on a smoking hot, ridged grill pan for 1–2 minutes, until lightly charred. Mix 2 tablespoons lemon juice with a pinch of ground sumac and 3 tablespoons olive oil and season to taste. Cut 1 orange into segments and toss with 5 cups arugula. Stir the dressing through the salad and arrange on a plate with the squid. Sprinkle with 1 finely chopped red chile to serve.

Squid Ink Risotto with Lemon

Heat 2 tablespoons olive oil in a saucepan, add 1 finely chopped onion, and cook for 5 minutes, until softened. Add 2 finely chopped garlic cloves and cook for 30 seconds. Add 1⅓ cups risotto rice and stir around the pan. Pour ½ cup dry white wine into the pan and cook until it has simmered away. Bring 1¾ cups fish or vegetable stock to a boil in a saucepan, then add 1 tablespoon squid ink. Gradually stir in the hot stock, a little at a time, stirring frequently and letting the rice absorb the stock before adding more. Meanwhile, heat 1 tablespoon olive oil in a skillet. Cut 5 oz squid into rings, season, and add to the skillet. Cook for 2 minutes, until lightly browned, then remove from the pan. When the rice is soft, after about 15 minutes, add the juice of 1 lemon and the cooked squid and serve sprinkled with a handful of chopped parsley.

Baked Mushrooms with Taleggio and Pesto

Serves 4

8 large flat mushrooms,
  stems trimmed
8 slices of Taleggio cheese
¾ cup dried bread crumbs
1 garlic clove, crushed
⅔ cup olive oil
bunch of basil leaves,
  finely chopped
¼ cup finely grated Parmesan
  cheese
3 tablespoons toasted pine nuts,
  chopped, plus extra to serve
salt and black pepper

· Put the mushrooms on a baking sheet and top each one with a slice of Taleggio. Mix together the bread crumbs and garlic and sprinkle a little over each mushroom. Drizzle with olive oil and bake in a preheated oven, at 400°F, for 15–20 minutes, until golden and crispy.

· Meanwhile, mix together the basil, Parmesan, pine nuts, and remaining oil and season to taste. Drizzle the pesto over the mushrooms and sprinkle with a few extra pine nuts to serve.

Mushroom Melts Heat 1 tablespoon oil in a nonstick skillet, add 2 cups sliced mushrooms, and cook for 3–5 minutes, until softened. Add 1 crushed garlic clove. Meanwhile, lightly toast 2 halved individual baguettes and arrange, cut side up, on a baking sheet. Spoon the mushrooms over the baguettes and top with 1 cup shredded cheddar cheese. Cook under a hot broiler for 2–3 minutes, until the cheese has melted, then drizzle with ¼ cup fresh pesto to serve.

Leek and Mushroom Casserole Heat 2 tablespoons oil in a skillet, add 1 thinly sliced leek and 2 cups sliced mushrooms, and cook for 3–5 minutes, until softened. Whisk 6 eggs with ¼ cup heavy cream and a handful of chopped basil and stir in the vegetables. Season and pour the mixture into a greased 8 inch square cake pan. Sprinkle with ¼ cup grated Parmesan cheese and bake in a preheated oven, at 350°F, for 25 minutes, until just set.

10 Spanish Shrimp with Chorizo

Serves 4

1 tablespoon olive oil
5 oz chorizo, thickly sliced
2 garlic cloves, sliced
8 oz large raw peeled shrimp
¼ cup dry sherry
handful of chopped parsley
salt and black pepper
crusty bread, to serve

- Heat the olive oil in a large skillet, add the chorizo, and cook for 1 minute on each side, until just golden and crisp. Remove from the skillet. Add the garlic and cook for 30 seconds. Then add the shrimp and cook for 3 minutes, until golden.

- Return the chorizo to the skillet and carefully pour in the sherry. Season to taste with salt and black pepper. Cook for 1 minute, then sprinkle with the parsley and serve with plenty of crusty bread.

20 Couscous Salad with Chorizo and Shrimp

In a large saucepan, heat 1 tablespoon olive oil, add 1 finely chopped onion, and cook for 5 minutes, until softened. Stir in 1 finely chopped garlic clove and cook for 30 seconds. Stir in 1 cup couscous and 1 cup canned rinsed and drained chickpeas (garbanzo beans), followed by 1¼ cups hot chicken stock. Remove the pan from the heat, cover, and let cool. Add 2 tablespoons lemon juice and 2 tablespoons olive oil, then stir in 4 oz cooked, peeled shrimp and 3 oz cooked, chopped chorizo. Season and add a large handful of chopped parsley before serving.

30 Garlicky Shrimp and Chorizo Pizza

Mix 1 (6½ oz) package of pizza crust mix according to the package directions and knead for 3 minutes. Roll out into a circle and let rise on a baking sheet lightly dusted with flour for 5 minutes. Spoon ½ cup fresh tomato pasta sauce over the top. Arrange 5 oz large cooked, peeled shrimp on top with 6 slices of chorizo. Mix together 1 crushed garlic clove with 1 tablespoon olive oil and drizzle over the top. Bake in a preheated oven, at 425°F, for 15 minutes or until crisp. Sprinkle with a handful of arugula leaves and serve.

Celeriac Remoulade with Prosciutto

Serves 6

⅓ cup mayonnaise
1 tablespoon Dijon mustard
2 tablespoons crème fraîche
  or sour cream
1 small celeriac, peeled and cut
  into fine matchsticks
handful of parsley, finely chopped
6 slices of prosciutto
salt and black pepper

· Mix together the mayonnaise, mustard, and crème fraîche until smooth. Season to taste, then stir together with the celeriac and parsley.

· Spoon the mixture onto serving plates along with the prosciutto.

---

2 **Celeriac Remoulade and Ham Rolls** Whisk together 2 egg yolks with 1 teaspoon Dijon mustard, then slowly whisk in 1¼ cups olive oil, at first one drop at a time, until creamy. Season to taste with lemon juice and salt and black pepper. Stir through 1 tablespoon drained capers and a handful each of chopped parsley and chives. Cut ½ celeriac into thin matchsticks and stir together with the mayonnaise. Spoon a little of the celeriac onto one end of a slice of ham and roll up, repeating to make 12 rolls. Arrange them on a plate with some arugula.

3 **Celeriac Soup with Crispy Prosciutto** Heat 1 tablespoon oil in a large saucepan, add 1 finely chopped onion, and cook for 5 minutes, until softened. Add 1 chopped celeriac and 1 chopped potato. Pour in 6⅓ cups chicken stock and add the finely grated rind of ½ lemon. Bring to a boil, then reduce the heat and simmer for 20 minutes, until soft. Use an immersion blender to blend to a smooth soup and season to taste. Meanwhile, heat 1 tablespoon oil in a small skillet, add 4 slices of prosciutto, and cook for 1–2 minutes, until just crispy. Add 2–3 sage leaves and sauté for 30 seconds, until crisp. Ladle the soup into bowls and top with some crumbled prosciutto and sage leaves and a sprinkling of finely grated Parmesan cheese.

 # Three Cheese Phyllo Bites

Serves 6

½ cup crumbled feta cheese
1 cup drained ricotta cheese
½ cup grated Pecorino cheese
2 eggs, beaten
1 stick butter, melted
¼ cup olive oil, plus extra
  for greasing
4 large sheets of phyllo pastry
salt and black pepper

- Mix the feta cheese together with the ricotta, Pecorino, and eggs. Season to taste. Stir together the butter and olive oil. Unwrap the phyllo pastry, keeping any pastry you are not using covered with a damp (but not wet) dish towel.

- Cut each pastry sheet into thirds lengthwise and brush all over with the butter mixture. Place a heaping spoonful of the cheese mixture at one end of a strip of pastry. Fold one corner of the pastry diagonally over the filling to meet the other side, then continue to fold all the way down the strip to create a triangular package. Repeat with the remaining pastry and ingredients.

- Place the packages on a lightly greased baking sheet, brush over again with the butter and oil, and bake in a preheated oven, at 400°F, for 12 minutes or until golden and crisp. Serve warm from the oven.

---

1 Fig and Cheese Crostini

Cut ½ baguette into slices and lightly toast. Mix together ½ cup ricotta with ½ cup crumbled feta cheese and spoon the mixture over the toasts. Slice 4 figs and arrange on top of the cheese. Use a vegetable peeler to shave a little Pecorino over each crostini to serve.

2 Tomato and Three Cheese Fritters

Mix together 1 cup drained ricotta with 1 beaten egg, 1 cup chopped sun-dried tomatoes, 1 crushed garlic clove, and ¼ cup finely grated Pecorino. Add ⅓ cup all-purpose flour and mix together. Heat a large, nonstick skillet, add a little olive oil, and then drop spoonfuls of the cheese batter into the skillet. Cook for 2 minutes on each side, until golden and cooked through. Arrange the fritters on plates with a handful of arugula leaves and sliced cucumber. Drizzle with 1 tablespoon olive oil and 2 teaspoons balsamic vinegar, then sprinkle with ⅓ cup crumbled feta and a handful of chopped fresh oregano.

 # Crispy Bacon Oysters

Serves 4

2 tablespoons olive oil

1 (6 oz) package baby spinach leaves

1 scallion, sliced

1 garlic clove, crushed

2 tablespoons crème fraîche or sour cream

4 slices of bacon

12 oysters

½ cup dried bread crumbs

pinch of cayenne

salt and black pepper

- Heat 1 tablespoon oil in a skillet, add the spinach leaves, and cook for 1 minute, until starting to wilt. Add the scallion and garlic and cook for another 1 minute, until wilted. Pour away any excess water, then stir in the crème fraîche.

- Meanwhile, cook the bacon for 5–8 minutes, until crisp, then cut into small pieces. Open the oysters, discarding the top shell, and arrange them on a baking sheet. Spoon some of the spinach mixture (together with any oyster juices) over the oysters and add some bacon pieces. Mix the bread crumbs with the cayenne and sprinkle over the top.

- Drizzle with the remaining oil and bake in a preheated oven, at 450°F, for 10 minutes or until the bread crumbs are crisp.

Smoked Oyster and Spinach Omelet

Heat a large skillet, add 4 cups baby spinach leaves and 1 sliced garlic clove, and cook for 2 minutes, until wilted. Remove from the skillet and wipe it clean. Whisk together 4 eggs and 1 egg yolk. Add one-quarter of the egg mixture to the skillet and swirl around. When it is just starting to set, sprinkle with one-quarter of the cooked spinach, one-quarter of a can of smoked oysters, drained, and a few pieces of sliced prosciutto. Roll up and repeat to make 4 omelets.

Spinach and Oyster Bisque

Heat 1 tablespoon oil in a large saucepan, add 2 slices of bacon, and cook for 5 minutes, until browned. Remove from the pan. Add 1 finely chopped onion and 1 finely chopped leek and cook over low heat for 5 minutes, until softened. Remove from the pan. Melt 2 tablespoons butter in the pan, then stir in 1 tablespoon all-purpose flour and cook for 2 minutes, stirring often. Pour in ⅔ cup vegetable stock, whisking together until smooth. Then whisk in another 6⅓ cups stock and a splash of Pernod, if liked. Return the vegetables to the pan and bring to a boil. Reduce the heat and simmer for 10 minutes. Shuck 12 oysters. Add 8 along with the juices to the soup together with 1 (12 oz) package baby spinach leaves. Cook for 1 minute, then blend in a food processor until smooth. Return to the pan and stir in ½ cup heavy cream and the bacon and heat through. Put the remaining oysters into serving bowls, ladle the soup over them, and serve immediately.

 # Asparagus Mimosa

Serves 4

6 quails' or 2 hens' eggs
8 oz asparagus
1 teaspoon Dijon mustard
1 tablespoon white wine vinegar
1 tablespoon light cream
⅓ cup olive oil
1 tablespoon capers, drained
½ cup chopped, pitted ripe
  black olives
salt and black pepper

- Bring a saucepan of water to a boil and gently lower in the eggs. Cook the quails' eggs for 5 minutes or the hens' eggs for 8 minutes. Remove from the pan and cool under cold running water. Cook the asparagus in a pan of lightly salted boiling water for 3–5 minutes, until just tender, drain, and cool under cold running water.

- Stir together the mustard, vinegar, and cream and then slowly whisk in the oil, a little at a time. Season well.

- Arrange the asparagus on 4 plates and drizzle with the dressing. Coarsely chop the eggs and sprinkle with the asparagus together with the capers and olives.

Asparagus with Soft Boiled Egg

Cook 1 cup asparagus tips in a saucepan of lightly salted boiling water for 2–3 minutes, until just tender and then remove from the pan. Bring the water back to a boil, add 4 eggs, and cook for 4 minutes, until soft boiled. Place in egg cups and slice off the tops. Wrap a strip of smoked salmon around each asparagus tip and use them to dip into the eggs.

Asparagus Tart

 Mix together 2 eggs with ⅔ cup mascarpone cheese and ⅔ cup grated Parmesan. Place a sheet of ready-to-bake puff pastry on a lightly greased baking sheet. Score a ½ inch border around the pastry. Spread the egg mixture all over the pastry, inside the border, then arrange 1⅓ cups asparagus spears on top together with ¼ cup coarsely chopped, pitted ripe black olives. Drizzle with

1 tablespoon olive oil and bake in a preheated oven, at 400°F, for 15–20 minutes, until golden and puffed.

Turkish Pizza with Spinach, Pomegranate, and Feta

Serves 4

2 (6½ oz) packages pizza crust mix

1 tablespoon olive oil, plus extra for greasing

2 garlic cloves, sliced

1 (6 oz) package baby spinach leaves

1 cup crumbled feta cheese

⅓ cup pomegranate seeds

salt and black pepper

- Mix the pizza crust according to the package directions and knead for 3 minutes. Divide the dough into 4 pieces, roll out each piece into an oval shape, and place on a lightly greased baking sheet. Let rise for 5–10 minutes.

- Meanwhile, heat the oil in a skillet, add the garlic, and cook for a couple of seconds. Add the spinach and cook for 3 minutes, until wilted. Season well and squeeze away any excess water.

- Arrange the spinach on the pizza crusts, leaving a ¾ inch border. Fold in the long edges of the pizza and twist the ends. Sprinkle with the feta and bake in a preheated oven, at 400°F, for 15–20 minutes, until the pizza is crisp and cooked through. Sprinkle with the pomegranate seeds before serving.

Spinach and Feta Salad with Pita Chips Split 2 pita breads open horizontally and cut each half into wedges. Brush all over with 2 tablespoons olive oil and place in a preheated oven, at 400°F, for 5–7 minutes or until golden and crisp. Whisk together 1 crushed garlic clove with 1 tablespoon white wine vinegar and 3 tablespoons olive oil. Toss together with 1 (5 oz) package baby spinach leaves. Transfer to serving plates and arrange the pita chips, ⅓ cup crumbled feta cheese, and 2 tablespoons pomegranate seeds on top.

Spinach and Feta Dip with Grilled Flatbreads Heat 1 tablespoon olive oil in a large saucepan, add 1 finely chopped onion, and cook for 5 minutes, until softened. Add 1 (6 oz) package baby spinach leaves to the saucepan with a splash of water. Cover and let cook, stirring ccasionally, for 2 minutes, until wilted. Squeeze away any water and let cool. Place in a food processor with 1 cup ricotta, 1⅓ cups feta cheese, 1 crushed garlic clove, and a squeeze of lemon juice and process until smooth. Brush 1 tablespoon olive oil over 4 large pita breads. Heat a ridged grill pan until smoking hot and cook the breads for 1–2 minutes on each side, until lightly charred. Serve with the dip.

1 Crab and Mango Salad with Chile Lime Dressing

Serves 4

¼ cup granulated sugar

⅓ cup water

2 tablespoons mirin
  (Japanese rice wine)

1 red chile, sliced

1 kaffir lime leaf, shredded

finely grated rind and juice of
  1 lime

1 mango, peeled, pitted,
  and chopped

⅔ cup halved radishes

¼ cucumber, sliced

1 bunch of watercress

8 oz freshly picked
  crabmeat

- Put the sugar, water, and mirin in a small saucepan, bring to a boil, and cook for 3 minutes, until it starts to turn syrupy. Stir in the chile, lime leaf, and lime rind and add lime juice to taste. Set aside for 5 minutes.

- Toss together the mango, radishes, cucumber, and watercress and arrange on serving plates. Sprinkle the crabmeat on top and then drizzle with the dressing.

2 Thai Crab Cakes with Mango Salsa

Mix together 1 lb freshly picked crabmeat with 2 teaspoons Thai red curry paste, 1 tablespoon Thai fish sauce, and just enough beaten egg white to bring the mixture together. Lightly wet your hands and shape into small patties. Heat 1 tablespoon oil in a nonstick skillet, add the crab cakes, and cook for 3 minutes on each side, until golden and just cooked through. Meanwhile, peel and finely chop the flesh of ½ mango and mix with 1 tablespoon finely chopped red onion, ½ finely chopped red chile, a good squeeze of lime juice, and a handful of chopped fresh cilantro. Spoon the salsa over the crab cakes to serve.

3 Wild Rice, Crab, and Mango Salad

Bring a large saucepan of lightly salted water to a boil, add 1 cup mixed wild rice and long-grain rice, and cook according to the package directions. Drain and rinse under cold running water to cool. Meanwhile, mix 1 tablespoon finely chopped red onion with 1 teaspoon finely chopped fresh ginger root, 1 finely chopped red chile, the juice and finely grated rind of 1 lime, and 3 tablespoons olive oil. Add the rice, a large handful of chopped fresh cilantro, 1 peeled and chopped mango, and 5 oz picked fresh crabmeat, stir well, and serve.

Whole Baked Brie with Pecans and Maple Syrup

Serves 4

1 (10 oz) whole baby Brie
  or Camembert
¼ cup pecans
3 tablespoons maple syrup
3 tablespoons packed light
  brown sugar
thyme sprigs
crusty bread, to serve

· Remove any plastic packaging from the cheese and return it to its wooden box. Place on a baking sheet and cook in a preheated oven, at 400°F, for 15 minutes.

· Meanwhile, toast the pecans in a small skillet for 3–5 minutes, until lightly browned, then set aside. Put the maple syrup and sugar in a small saucepan and bring to a boil. Cook for 1 minute, until foamy.

· Take the cheese from the oven and cut a small cross in the center. Drizzle with the maple syrup, sprinkle with the pecans and thyme, and serve with plenty of crusty bread.

Brie Salad with Maple Dressing Whisk together 1 tablespoon maple syrup with 1 teaspoon mustard, 1 tablespoon white wine vinegar, and 3 tablespoons olive oil. Season and toss together with 7 cups mixed salad greens. Arrange on plates with ¼ cup toasted pecans. Cut 4 oz Brie into thick slices. Put the Brie on a baking sheet and cook under a hot broiler for 1 minute or until starting to melt. Sprinkle with the salad to serve.

Brie en Croûte with Cranberries, Maple Syrup, and Pecans Slice a whole (10 oz) baby Brie in half horizontally. Sprinkle ¼ cup dried cranberries and a handful of chopped pecans over one half, then drizzle with 2 tablespoons maple syrup. Put the other half back on top. Cut out 2 circles from a sheet of ready-to-bake puff pastry, one slightly larger than the other, to accommodate the Brie. Put the Brie on the smaller circle and brush the pastry edges with 1 beaten egg. Put the other pastry circle on top and press together the edges with your fingers. Brush over more egg and cook in a preheated oven, at 425°F, for 10 minutes. Turn the oven down to 350°F and cook for another 10–15 minutes, until puffed and golden.

 # Crispy Tostados with Avocado and Tomatoes

Serves 4

4 corn tortillas
1 tablespoon vegetable oil
2 avocados, peeled and pitted
¼ cup crème fraîche
  or sour cream
2–3 tablespoons lime juice
4 tomatoes, chopped
1 tablespoon finely chopped
  red onion
1 tablespoon extra virgin olive oil
handful of fresh cilantro,
  chopped, plus extra to serve
  (optional)
salt and black pepper

- Use a 2 inch cookie cutter to stamp out circles from the tortillas; alternatively, cut them into wedges. Brush them with vegetable oil, place on a baking sheet under a preheated hot broiler, and cook for 1 minute on each side, until crisp. Let cool.

- Meanwhile, place the avocado flesh and crème fraîche in a food processor and blend until smooth. Stir in 1 tablespoon of lime juice and season to taste. Stir together the tomatoes, onion, and olive oil, add lime juice to taste, season, and stir through the cilantro. Spoon a little of the avocado mixture onto each tortilla circle, sprinkle with the tomato salsa, and top with more cilantro, if liked.

 Crispy Baked Avocado with Tomatoes Slice 2 avocados in half and remove the pits. Scoop out the flesh, setting aside the shells, and coarsely mash. Cook 2 slices of bacon for 5–7 minutes, until just crisp, then chop into small pieces. Stir through the avocado with 1 chopped tomato and a handful of chopped cilantro. Spoon the mixture into the shells and place on a baking sheet. Sprinkle with ½ cup shredded cheddar cheese and 1 cup crushed corn tortilla chips. Bake in a preheated oven, at 400°F, for 10 minutes or until the cheese has melted.

Tomato and Tortilla Soup Heat 1 tablespoon olive oil in a saucepan, add 1 finely chopped onion, and cook for 5 minutes, until softened. Add 3 finely chopped garlic cloves and stir around the pan. Add 2 teaspoons chipotle paste, 1 (14½ oz) can diced tomatoes, 1 teaspoon packed brown sugar, and a pinch of dried oregano. Pour in 4 cups chicken or vegetable stock, bring to a boil, reduce the heat, and simmer for 10 minutes. Use an immersion blender to blend together until smooth, then season to taste. Cut 2 corn tortillas into thin strips. Heat a large skillet, add 1 tablespoon vegetable oil, and cook the tortillas for 1–2 minutes, until golden and crisp. Spoon the soup into bowls. Top with the chopped flesh of 1 avocado, ⅓ cup crumbled feta cheese, the crisp tortillas, and a handful of chopped fresh cilantro.

 Clam Pasta with Tomatoes

Serves 4

3 tablespoons olive oil
2 garlic cloves, sliced
finely grated rind and juice of
  ½ lemon
3 canned anchovy fillets
½ cup dry white wine
pinch of dried red pepper flakes
8 halved cherry tomatoes
1 lb clams, scrubbed
1 lb fresh spaghetti
3 cups arugula
salt and black pepper

- Heat the olive oil in a large saucepan, add the garlic, lemon rind, and anchovy to the pan, and cook for 30 seconds, mashing the anchovy lightly so it dissolves into the sauce. Pour in the wine and let simmer for a couple of minutes. Add the red pepper flakes, tomatoes, and clams to the pan. Cover with a lid and heat for 5 minutes, until the clams have opened, discarding any that do not open. Add a tablespoon of lemon juice to the pan and season with pepper.

- Meanwhile, heat a large saucepan of lightly salted water until boiling and then add the spaghetti. Cook according to the package directions, drain, reserving a little of the cooking water, and return to the pan.

- Stir through the clams and any juices with a little cooking water to loosen, if necessary, then toss through the arugula just before serving.

---

2 **Clam and Tomato Soup with Arugula Dressing**

Heat 2 tablespoons olive oil in a saucepan, add 1 chopped onion, and cook for 5 minutes, until softened. Add 2 finely chopped garlic cloves and cook for another 30 seconds. Pour in ¾ cup canned tomatoes and 5 cups chicken or vegetable stock. Let simmer for 5 minutes. Add 12 oz clams and cook for 5 minutes, discarding any that do not open. Meanwhile, blend together 3 cups arugula leaves with ¼ cup olive oil. Swirl over the soup before serving.

3 **Tomato Baked Clams**

Heat ½ cup dry white wine in a saucepan. Add 1 lb clams, cover, and steam for 5 minutes. Discard any that do not open and let cool for a couple of minutes. Reserve the cooking liquid. Remove the meat from the clams and set aside. Break apart the clam shells and place 12 of the most attractive halves on a baking sheet. Heat 2 tablespoons olive oil in a saucepan, add 1 finely chopped shallot, and cook for 3 minutes. Stir in 1 crushed garlic clove, then add 2 chopped tomatoes. Pour in the clam cooking liquid and cook for 5 minutes, until the liquid has boiled away. Stir in the clam meat, a squeeze of lemon juice, a handful of finely chopped arugula, and 3 cups fresh bread crumbs. Spoon the mixture into the clam shells and drizzle with a little more oil. Cook under a hot broiler for 3–5 minutes, until golden and crisp.

Salmon Carpaccio with Beet Topping

Serves 4

1 lb piece of really fresh skinless, boneless salmon

½ cup crème fraîche or sour cream

1–2 tablespoons horseradish sauce

squeeze of lemon juice

finely grated rind of ½ orange

1 tablespoon olive oil

3 cups salad greens

2 cooked beets (not preserved in vinegar), chopped

salt and black pepper

- Trim any brown flesh from the salmon and slice it thinly. Place the slices between 2 pieces of plastic wrap, leaving plenty of space between, then use a mallet or rolling pin to pound the salmon gently until it is thin but not mushy.

- Mix together the crème fraîche and horseradish to taste. Arrange the salmon slices on plates.

- Toss together the lemon juice, orange rind, and olive oil with the salad greens and beets and season to taste. Arrange the salad on top of the salmon and drizzle with the crème fraîche to serve.

1 Smoked Salmon Bites with Beet

Salad Mix together ⅓ cup crème fraîche or sour cream with 1 tablespoon horseradish sauce. Arrange 4 slices of smoked salmon in little nest shapes in the center of 4 serving plates. Place a little of the horseradish inside each. Whisk together 1 tablespoon red wine vinegar with 3 tablespoons olive oil and mix with 5 cups salad greens. Add 2 chopped, cooked beets. Arrange around the salmon and sprinkle with black pepper and snipped dill before serving.

3 Smoked Salmon and Beet Bites

Line 4 individual ramekins with plastic wrap. Carefully place a large slice of smoked salmon in each ramekin, draping the ends over the sides of the ramekins. Coarsely chop 7 oz smoked salmon and mix together with 1 small chopped beet. Stir in 2 tablespoons crème fraîche or sour cream, the finely grated rind of ½ lemon, and 1 tablespoon lemon juice. Fill the ramekins with the mixture, folding the salmon slices over the top so the filling is completely enclosed. Place in the refrigerator for 15–20 minutes, until firm. Invert each salmon bite onto a plate and serve with a green salad.

30 Blue Cheese Soufflé with Apple and Arugula

Serves 6

3 slices crustless sourdough
    bread, cut into chunks
1 cup milk
5 oz blue cheese
4 tablespoons butter, softened,
    plus extra for greasing
4 eggs, separated
1 tablespoon white wine vinegar
3 tablespoons olive oil
1 teaspoon walnut oil
1 red apple, cored and thinly sliced
handful of arugula leaves
salt and black pepper

- Put the bread in a bowl and pour over the milk. Let rest for 5 minutes, then squeeze any excess milk from the bread. Transfer the bread to a food processor with the cheese, butter, and egg yolks and process until smooth. Season to taste. Whisk the egg whites until stiff peaks form. Stir a large spoonful into the cheese mixture, then carefully fold in the remainder, half at a time.

- Spoon the mixture into 6 well-buttered ramekins, each holding about ¾ cup, and bake in a preheated oven, at 425°F, for 10–15 minutes, until puffed and golden.

- Meanwhile, whisk together the white wine vinegar, olive oil, and walnut oil and season to taste. Toss together with the apple and arugula leaves and serve alongside the soufflés.

---

1 Blue Cheese Waldorf Salad

Mash 3 oz blue cheese together with ⅓ cup mayonnaise. Stir together with 3 chopped apples, 6 chopped celery sticks, 2 sliced scallions, and ½ cup toasted chopped walnuts. Place in a serving dish and sprinkle with some more walnuts, blue cheese, and celery leaves to serve.

2 Baked Mushrooms with Blue Cheese Soufflé Topping

Put 6 portobello mushrooms on a baking sheet. Stir together 6 oz blue cheese and ⅓ cup crème fraîche or sour cream until smooth, then mix in 3 egg yolks and a handful of finely chopped thyme. Whisk 3 egg whites until stiff peaks form. Carefully fold into the cheese mixture. Spoon a little of the mixture on top of each mushroom and cook in a preheated oven, at 425°F, for 12 minutes or until golden and puffed.

Caesar Salad

Serves 4

½ baguette, torn into chunks
2 tablespoons olive oil
12 quails' eggs
1 garlic clove, crushed
2 canned anchovy fillets, minced
2 tablespoons crème fraîche
   or sour cream
1 teaspoon Dijon mustard
¼ cup extra virgin olive oil
¼ cup grated Parmesan cheese,
   plus extra shavings to serve
lemon juice, to taste
2 baby romaine lettuce,
   leaves separated
black pepper

- Toss the baguette chunks with the olive oil, transfer to a baking sheet, and bake in a preheated oven, at 400°F, for 7–10 minutes, until golden and crisp. Let cool. Carefully lower the eggs into a saucepan of boiling water and cook for 5 minutes, then cool under cold running water. Shell and halve.

- Mix together the garlic, anchovies, crème fraîche, and mustard, then slowly whisk in the olive oil. Stir through the grated Parmesan, season with black pepper, and stir in lemon juice to taste.

- Arrange the salad greens on plates along with the baguette chunks and eggs. Drizzle with the sauce and sprinkle with the Parmesan shavings to serve.

---

10 Open Chicken Caesar Sandwich

Mash 1 canned anchovy fillet and mix together with ¼ cup mayonnaise, a handful of grated Parmesan, and 1 tablespoon lemon juice. Spread over 4 slices of lightly toasted bread and top with 1 baby romaine lettuce, coarsely chopped. Place 2 sliced, cooked chicken breasts on top and grate a little more Parmesan over the sandwiches to finish.

---

30 Caesar Salad with Poached Eggs and Fresh Mayonnaise Whisk 2 egg yolks with 1 teaspoon Dijon mustard, 2 finely chopped canned anchovy fillets, and 1 crushed garlic clove. Slowly whisk in 1¼ cups olive oil, a drop at a time to start with. When the mixture is thick and creamy, stir in 3 tablespoons crème fraîche or sour cream and ¼ cup grated Parmesan. Season to taste with lemon juice and salt and black pepper. Cut ½ sourdough loaf into slices, brush with olive oil, and cook on a smoking hot, ridged grill pan for 2–3 minutes on each side, until charred and lightly crisp. Heat a saucepan of water and 1 tablespoon white wine vinegar until boiling. Reduce the heat to a low simmer and make a whirlpool in the center of the pan by stirring vigorously with a spoon. Crack an egg into a cup and slip it into the middle of the whirlpool. Cook for 4 minutes and remove with a slotted spoon. Repeat to poach 4 eggs. Toss 2 sliced baby romaine lettuce with the dressing and arrange on plates with the bread, cut into chunks. Return the eggs to the pan for 30 seconds to reheat and serve on top of the salad, sprinkled with grated Parmesan.

Baked Feta with Watermelon

Serves 4

8 oz feta cheese
⅓ cup extra virgin olive oil
8 oz watermelon, sliced
¾ cup chopped pitted
  Kalamata olives
pinch of dried red pepper flakes
handful of mint leaves

- Tear off a large sheet of aluminum foil. Place the feta on the foil and drizzle with 1 tablespoon of oil. Fold over the edges of the foil to enclose, transfer to a baking sheet, and cook in a preheated oven, at 375°F, for 12 minutes.

- Arrange the remaining ingredients on serving plates, crumble the warm feta over the top, then drizzle with the remaining oil.

1 Watermelon and Feta Salad

Whisk together 1 tablespoon white wine vinegar with 3 tablespoons extra virgin olive oil and a pinch of red pepper flakes. Toss together with 2 chopped tomatoes, 1½ cups chopped watermelon, and a handful of arugula leaves and arrange on 4 serving plates. Sprinkle with 1 cup crumbled feta cheese to serve.

3 Feta Bites with Watermelon

Salsa Stir together 1⅓ cups crumbled feta cheese with ½ cup mascarpone cheese and 1 tablespoon beaten egg. Cut 4 sheets of phyllo pastry in half to make 8 squares. Cover the pastry with a damp but not wet layer of paper towels. Lay one sheet in front of you and spoon a little of the feta mixture on one end. Brush around the edges with beaten egg. Fold in the 2 long sides, then tightly roll up the package, making sure it is completely enclosed. Repeat with the remaining rolls. Heat a large, deep saucepan one-third full of oil until a piece of bread crisps and browns in 15 seconds. Cook the rolls, in batches, for 2–3 minutes, until golden and crisp and keep warm. Mix 1 cup finely chopped watermelon with 1 minced chile, 1 tablespoon finely chopped red onion, and a large handful of chopped mint. Serve in a bowl alongside the feta bites.

FOO-STAR-ZIG

Red Pepper Dip with Herb Pita Crackers

Serves 4

⅓ cup olive oil

1 shallot, finely chopped

1 cup walnut halves

1 cup roasted red peppers

1 garlic clove, crushed

1 teaspoon ground cumin

1 tablespoon pomegranate
molasses (availabe in Middle
Eastern or gourmet stores)
or pomegranate juice

4 pita breads

handful of chopped parsley

handful of chopped mint

coarse sea salt

- Heat 1 tablespoon oil in a skillet, add the shallot, and cook for 3 minutes, until softened. Let cool. Toast the walnut halves in a dry skillet for 3 minutes, until lightly browned and let cool. Put the walnuts in a blender with the shallot, roasted peppers, garlic, cumin, pomegranate molasses, and 2 tablespoons oil and blend together until smooth. Season to taste.

- Meanwhile, split the pita breads open horizontally and cut each half into wedges. Mix together the remaining oil with the herbs and brush over the wedges. Place on a baking sheet, sprinkle with coarse sea salt, and bake in a preheated oven, at 375°F, for 5–7 minutes or until golden and crisp. Serve alongside the red pepper dip.

Herb and Roasted Pepper Salad

Lightly toast ¼ cup walnut halves in a dry skillet. Whisk 1 tablespoon sherry vinegar with 3 tablespoons olive oil. Toss with 5 cups mixed herb greens and 2 roasted red peppers, cut into strips. Season to taste. Arrange on a plate, then sprinkle with the walnuts and ⅓ cup crumbled soft goat cheese.

Herbed Couscous Stuffed Red

Peppers Put ½ cup couscous in a bowl, pour in ½ cup hot vegetable stock, cover, and let sit for 5 minutes, until soft. Stir through 3 tablespoons olive oil, 2 chopped tomatoes, 1 teaspoon balsamic vinegar, and a large handful each of chopped mint and parsley. Season to taste. Meanwhile, halve 2 red peppers lengthwise and remove the cores and seeds. Place the peppers on a baking sheet and spoon the couscous mixture into the cavities. Drizzle with 1 tablespoon olive oil and cook in a preheated oven, at 400°F, for 20–25 minutes or until the peppers are just soft.

Spiced Mussels in a Coconut Broth

Serves 4

1 tablespoon vegetable oil
1 shallot, finely chopped
1 garlic clove, sliced
1 red chile, chopped
2 lime leaves, shredded
½ cup coconut milk
½ cup water
1 lemon grass stalk
1 tablespoon Thai fish sauce
1 tablespoon packed light
   brown sugar
2 lb mussels, scrubbed
handful of fresh cilantro, chopped

- Heat the oil in a large saucepan, add the shallot, and cook for 2 minutes. Stir in the garlic, chile, and lime leaves and cook for another 1 minute. Pour in the coconut milk and the measured water, add the lemon grass, fish sauce, and sugar, and let simmer for 10 minutes.

- Add the mussels, cover, and cook for 3–5 minutes, until the mussels are open, discarding any that do not open. Sprinkle with the cilantro to serve.

Spicy Wok-Roasted Mussels

Heat 1 tablespoon vegetable oil in a large wok, add 1 tablespoon Thai green curry paste, and cook for 1 minute. Add 2 lb cleaned mussels and cook for 1 minute. Pour in ¼ cup coconut milk, cover, and cook for another 2 minutes, until the mussels are open, discarding any that do not open. Sprinkle with 1 chopped scallion, a handful of chopped fresh cilantro, and 1 tablespoon lime juice to serve.

Spicy Seafood Soup

Heat 1 tablespoon vegetable oil in a large saucepan, add 1 tablespoon Thai red curry paste and a pinch of turmeric, and cook for 1 minute. Add 1¾ cups canned coconut milk, ¾ inch piece of fresh ginger root, 2 lime leaves, and 2½ cups chicken stock. Bring to a boil, reduce the heat, and let simmer for 15 minutes. Remove the ginger and lime leaves. Add 5 oz large, raw peeled shrimp and 1 lb cleaned mussels and cook for 3 minutes, until just cooked through. Remove any mussels that do not open. Meanwhile, cook 6 oz rice noodles according to the package directions. Add to the soup along with 4 oz squid cut into rings and heat for 1 minute, until the squid is cooked through. Serve sprinkled with a handful of bean sprouts and some chopped mint and cilantro leaves.

Chicken Liver Pâté

Serves 6

1 tablespoon olive oil
1 shallot, finely chopped
8 oz chicken livers
½ cup dessert wine
1 cup heavy cream
½ baguette, thinly sliced
salt and black pepper

To serve

red onion, finely chopped
capers

- Heat the oil in a skillet, add the shallot, and cook for 3 minutes, until softened. Wash the chicken livers and trim away any sinews. Pat dry and add to the skillet. Season to taste and cook until browned all over but still soft to the touch. Pour in the wine and cook for 5 minutes. Add the cream and cook for another 5–10 minutes, until reduced by half. Blend in a food processor until smooth, then check and adjust the seasoning, if necessary. If you want it extra smooth, press the mixture through a strainer. Transfer to a serving bowl and let cool to room temperature.

- Meanwhile, toast the baguette slices until golden and crisp and let cool. Serve alongside the pâté with some finely chopped red onion and capers for sprinkling over, if liked.

Seared Liver Toasts with Creamy Marsala Sauce Heat 2 tablespoons olive oil in a heavy saucepan and add 1 lb trimmed and cleaned chicken livers with 1 sliced shallot. Cook for about 5 minutes, until golden all over. Pour in ⅓ cup Marsala wine and let cook for 3 minutes, until reduced down. Stir in 3 tablespoons heavy cream, season to taste, and warm through. Lightly toast 6 slices of brioche. Spoon the livers and sauce over the toast, sprinkle with chopped parsley, and serve.

Chopped Chicken Liver and Eggs Heat 1 tablespoon oil in a saucepan, add 1 chopped onion, and cook over low heat for 10 minutes, until soft. Heat another tablespoon of oil in a skillet and cook 1 lb trimmed chicken livers for 8 minutes, until golden and just cooked through. Let cool. Put the onion and liver in a food processor and pulse to make a coarse purée. Stir in 4 chopped hard-boiled eggs and season to taste. Cool and serve with toasted challah bread or crackers.

Fava Bean and Pea Crostini

Serves 6

⅓ cup olive oil
1 lemon
2 garlic cloves, peeled
2 cups shelled fava beans
2 cups peas
6 slices of sourdough bread
handful of mint leaves
salt and black pepper

To serve

2 radishes, thinly sliced
handful of pea shoots
Pecorino cheese shavings

- Put the oil, 3 strips of lemon rind, and the garlic cloves in a small saucepan and cook over low heat for 7–10 minutes. Remove from the heat and discard the lemon rind.

- Cook the fava beans and peas in a saucepan of lightly salted boiling water for 3 minutes, until just soft. Drain and rinse under cold running water to cool. Peel the fava beans.

- Tip most of the peas and beans into a blender, add the mint and cooked garlic together with the flavored oil, and pulse to make a coarse puree. Season well.

- Toast the bread, halve the slices, and arrange on a serving platter. Spread with the puree and sprinkle with the reserved peas and fava beans. Top with radishes, pea shoots, and Pecorino cheese shavings and serve.

Pea and Fava Bean Salad

Cook ⅔ cup each of peas and shelled fava beans in lightly salted boiling water for 3 minutes, until soft, drain, and cool under cold running water. Whisk 3 tablespoons olive oil with 1 tablespoon lemon juice, season, and toss with 5 cups salad greens. Place on serving plates, sprinkle with the peas and beans, and top with Pecorino cheese shavings to serve.

Pea and Fava Bean Soup

Heat 1 tablespoon olive oil in a saucepan, add 1 finely chopped onion, and cook for 5 minutes, until softened. Add 3 oz diced bacon and cook for another 5 minutes, until browned. Stir in 1 crushed garlic clove and cook for 1 minute, until soft. Stir in 1 tablespoon all-purpose flour and cook for 2 minutes, then stir in ⅓ cup dry white wine. Cook for 5 minutes, until reduced, then pour in 6 cups chicken or vegetable stock and let simmer for 10 minutes. Stir in 1 cup fine asparagus tips and 1⅓ cups each of peas and shelled fava beans and cook for 3 minutes, until soft. Divide the soup among 6 bowls, sprinkle with a handful of mint leaves and some Pecorino shavings, and serve with toasted sourdough bread.

QuickCook
Meat and Poultry

Recipes listed by cooking time

3⃝

2⃝

Roasted Chicken Breasts with Herb Butter

Serves 4

4 tablespoons butter, softened
grated rind of 1 lemon
1 garlic clove, crushed
handful of basil, finely chopped
4 skinless, boneless chicken
  breasts
⅓ cup olive oil, plus extra for
  greasing
1 cup dry bread crumbs
¼ cup grated Parmesan cheese
salt and black pepper

To serve

new potatoes
green beans

- Mix together the butter, lemon rind, garlic, and basil and season to taste. Use a sharp knife to make a small horizontal slit in the side of each chicken breast to form a little pocket, making sure you don't cut all the way through the meat. Tuck some of the butter inside each breast, then smooth over to seal.

- Rub 1 tablespoon oil over each chicken breast and season well. Put the bread crumbs on a plate and dip each breast in the crumbs until well coated.

- Transfer the chicken to a lightly greased baking pan, sprinkle with the Parmesan, drizzle with the remaining oil, and cook in a preheated oven, at 400°F, for 15 minutes or until golden and cooked through. Serve with new potatoes and green beans.

Herbed Chicken Sandwiches

Mix together ⅓ cup mayonnaise, the finely grated rind of ½ lemon, and a handful of chopped basil. Cut 4 chicken breasts into slices, season, and rub with 2 tablespoons oil. Cook on a preheated ridged grill pan for 5 minutes, turning once, until seared and cooked through. Spread the mayonnaise on the cut sides of 4 split ciabatta rolls and fill with the warm chicken and some salad greens.

Herb Butter Chicken Kievs

Mix together 4 tablespoons softened butter, the grated rind of 1 lemon, 1 crushed garlic clove, and a handful of finely chopped basil. Season to taste and use to fill 4 skinless, boneless chicken breasts as in the first step of the main recipe. Sprinkle ⅓ cup flour on a plate. Pour 1 lightly beaten egg onto a second plate and spread 1 cup dry bread crumbs on a third. Dip the chicken in the flour, dusting off any excess, then in the egg, and finally in the bread crumbs. Heat a large skillet and add ⅓ cup vegetable oil. Cook the chicken for 3 minutes on each side, until golden. Remove from the skillet and pat with paper towels. Place on a baking sheet and cook in a preheated oven, at 350°F, for 15–20 minutes, until cooked through. Serve with a green salad and potato wedges.

Chicken, Leek, and Tarragon Pie

Serves 4

2 leeks, thinly sliced
8 roasted chicken legs, bones
    removed and meat coarsely
    chopped
4 oz thick piece of ham, cubed
⅔ cup crème fraîche
    or heavy cream
handful of tarragon leaves,
    chopped
1 sheet store-bought rolled
    dough pie crust
1 egg, lightly beaten
salt and black pepper

To serve

peas
mashed potatoes

- Put the leeks in a strainer or colander and pour over boiling water until starting to wilt. Mix the leeks together with the chicken meat, ham, crème fraîche, and tarragon and season. Transfer the mixture to a 9 inch pie plate.

- Place the dough on top, crimp around the edges, and cut away any excess dough. Make a small slit in the center of the dough and brush all over with the egg. Cook in a preheated oven, at 425°F, for 20–25 minutes, until golden and bubbling. Serve with peas and mashed potatoes.

10 Chicken, Tarragon, and Bacon Salad

Cook 4 bacon slices under a preheated hot broiler for 7 minutes, turning once, until crisp. Mix 1 cup plain yogurt, ¼ cup mayonnaise, 1 tablespoon whole-grain mustard, and a handful of chopped tarragon and season to taste. Combine with 3 sliced roasted chicken breasts. Toss the leaves from 1 lettuce and 1 head of endive with 3 tablespoons olive oil and 1 tablespoon white wine vinegar. Arrange on a plate with ⅔ cup sliced radishes. Top with the chicken and crumble the bacon over the top to serve.

20 Seared Chicken in Tarragon Bacon

Sauce Heat 1 tablespoon oil in a large skillet. Add 4 skinless, boneless chicken breasts, season, and cook for 7 minutes. Turn over and cook for another 5 minutes or until golden and cooked through. Remove from the skillet and keep warm. Add 2 oz chopped bacon and 1 finely chopped shallot and cook for 3 minutes, until softened. Pour in ½ cup dry white wine. Boil for a few minutes, until reduced by half, then whisk in 4 tablespoons cold butter cut into cubes to form a sauce. Add 1 tablespoon lemon juice and a handful of chopped tarragon, then spoon over the chicken. Serve with green beans and mashed potatoes.

Saffron Roasted Chicken

Serves 4

3 tablespoons milk
pinch of saffron threads
⅓ cup plain yogurt
2 garlic cloves, crushed
2 teaspoons finely grated fresh
   ginger root
¼ cup ground almonds
2 teaspoons toasted cumin seeds
4 chicken breasts
1 tablespoon butter, plus extra
   for greasing
¼ cup slivered almonds
handful of mint leaves
1 green chile, seeded and
   chopped
salt and black pepper

To serve
tomato salad
plain boiled rice

- Heat the milk, add the saffron, and set aside. Mix together the yogurt, garlic, ginger, ground almonds, and cumin seeds and season well. Coat the chicken in the mixture, place on a lightly greased baking sheet, and cook in a preheated oven, at 425°F, for 10 minutes.

- Pour the saffron liquid over the chicken, dot with the butter, and sprinkle with the slivered almonds, then cook for another 5 minutes or until the chicken is cooked through. Sprinkle with the mint leaves and chile and serve with a tomato salad and boiled rice.

 Chicken Chapatti Wraps

Mix 10 oz chicken strips with 2 tablespoons plain yogurt, a pinch of saffron threads, 1 teaspoon ground cumin, and a pinch of dried red pepper flakes. Season to taste and drizzle with 1 tablespoon oil. Heat a griddle pan until smoking and cook the chicken for 3–4 minutes on each side, until cooked through. Place on 4 warm chapattis and top with chopped tomatoes, sliced butterhead lettuce leaves, and some chopped fresh cilantro.

Saffron Chicken Pilaf

Heat 1 tablespoon oil in a skillet, add 4 boneless chicken thighs cut into chunks, and cook for 5–7 minutes, until golden all over. Melt 2 tablespoons butter in a large saucepan, add 1 tablespoon oil, and cook 1 finely chopped onion for 5 minutes. Add 2 finely chopped garlic cloves, 2 teaspoons grated fresh ginger root, 2 teaspoons cumin seeds, and 1 teaspoon coriander seeds and cook for 1 minute. Stir in 1½ cups basmati or other long-grain rice and a pinch of saffron threads. Return the chicken to the pan, then pour in 3¾ cups chicken stock. Season to taste, bring to a boil, and cook for 10 minutes. Lower the heat, cover the pan, and cook for another 5 minutes, until the chicken is cooked through and the rice is tender. Grate ½ cucumber and mix with the finely grated rind of 1 lime, 1 tablespoon lime juice, 1 crushed garlic clove, and ½ cup plain yogurt. Season to taste, stir in chopped mint, and serve with the pilaf.

Chicken and Chermoula Pilaf

Serves 6

¼ cup olive oil

finely grated rind and juice of
  1 lemon

2 teaspoons ground cumin

large handful of fresh cilantro,
  chopped

large handful of parsley, chopped

6 small chicken breasts, thickly
  sliced

1 onion, finely chopped

1 garlic clove, crushed

2 cups bulgur wheat

2 cups hot chicken stock

1 tablespoon pomegranate
  molasses or pomegranate juice

seeds from 1 pomegranate

salt and black pepper

- Mix together 2 tablespoons olive oil with half the grated lemon rind and juice, 1 teaspoon cumin, and a little cilantro and parsley. Rub all over the chicken and let marinate for 5–10 minutes.

- Heat 1 tablespoon oil in a large saucepan. Add the onion and cook for 5 minutes, until softened. Stir in the garlic and cook for 30 seconds. Add the remaining cumin, then stir in the bulgur wheat and cook for 1 minute. Pour in the stock, cover, and let simmer for 15 minutes or until all the liquid has been absorbed.

- Meanwhile, heat a small skillet and toast the walnuts for 3–5 minutes, then remove from the skillet and set aside. Heat a ridged grill pan until smoking, add the chicken, and cook for 3–5 minutes on each side, until charred and cooked through. Mix together the remaining oil, the pomegranate molasses, and the remaining lemon juice and rind. Toss through the bulgur along with the chicken, pomegranate seeds, and the remaining herbs.

---

1   Chicken Couscous Salad

Put 2 cups couscous into a bowl. Pour in 2 cups hot chicken stock, cover, and let sit for 5 minutes. Fluff the grains with a fork, then add 4 roasted chicken breasts, torn into strips, 3 tablespoons olive oil, the juice and finely grated rind of 1 lemon, 1 cup rinsed and drained canned chickpeas, ½ cup chopped olives, and a large handful of chopped fresh cilantro.

2   Chicken Stew with Bulgur Wheat

Heat 2 tablespoons olive oil in a large flameproof casserole or Dutch oven. Cook 6 skinless, boneless chicken breasts for 2–3 minutes on each side, until golden, then remove from the dish. Add 1 finely chopped onion and cook for 5 minutes, until softened. Stir in 1 crushed garlic clove, 2 teaspoons ground cumin, ½ finely chopped green chile, a pinch of saffron threads, and a large handful each of chopped fresh cilantro and parsley. Add the juice and finely grated rind of 1 lemon and ½ cup water and simmer for 2 minutes. Return the chicken to the dish and cook for 5–10 minutes, until cooked through. Serve with steamed bulgur wheat.

 # Spicy Stir-Fried Chicken

Serves 4

1 lb chicken breast, sliced
3 tablespoons light soy sauce
3 tablespoons rice wine
1 tablespoon cornstarch
3 tablespoons vegetable oil
½ cup cashew nuts
2 scallions, sliced
3 garlic cloves, sliced
1 tablespoon grated fresh
 ginger root
1 teaspoon chili sauce
2 teaspoons granulated sugar
3–4 tablespoons water

To serve

boiled rice
wilted watercress or arugula

- Mix together the chicken with 1 tablespoon each soy sauce and rice wine and 1 teaspoon cornstarch. Let marinate for 5–10 minutes.

- Heat 1 tablespoon oil in a wok or large skillet, add the cashew nuts, and stir around the skillet for 2 minutes, until lightly browned, then remove from the skillet. Heat the remaining oil and cook the chicken for 5–7 minutes, until just cooked through. Remove from the skillet.

- Add the scallions, garlic, and ginger and cook for 30 seconds, then return the chicken and nuts to the skillet, stir in the remaining soy sauce, rice wine, and cornstarch, the chili sauce, granulated sugar, and measured water. Heat until bubbling and slightly thickened. Serve with boiled rice and wilted watercress.

Spicy Chicken Skewers

Cut 2 large chicken breasts into long thin strips and thread onto metal skewers. Mix together 1 tablespoon each chili sauce and vegetable oil with 2 tablespoons soy sauce and rub over the chicken. Cook on a smoking ridged grill pan for 3–4 minutes on each side, until just cooked through. Serve with cooked rice noodles tossed together with 2 tablespoons each soy sauce and rice wine and ¼ cucumber, thinly sliced.

Lemon Chile Pilaf with Seared

Chicken Heat 2 tablespoons oil in a large saucepan, add 1 finely chopped onion, and cook for 5 minutes, until softened. Add 2 finely chopped garlic cloves and 2 teaspoons grated fresh roor ginger and cook for 30 seconds. Stir in ½ seeded and chopped chile, the finely grated rind of 1 lemon, and 1½ cups basmati or other long-grain rice. Pour in 2¾ cups chicken stock and season to taste. Let simmer for 10 minutes, then reduce the

heat to low, cover, and cook for 5 minutes, until the rice is soft. Stir in ¼ cup toasted cashew nuts. Meanwhile, cut 1 red bell pepper into strips and toss with 8 boneless, skinless chicken thighs, 2 tablespoons soy sauce, 1 tablespoon vegetable oil, and 2 tablespoons lemon juice. Heat a ridged grill pan until smoking and cook the chicken for 5 minutes, turn over, add the bell peppers, and cook for another 5–7 minutes, until charred and cooked through. Serve the chicken with the pilaf.

 # Chicken Saltimbocca

Serves 4

4 chicken breasts
8 slices of prosciutto
8 sage leaves

To serve

green beans
new potatoes

- Use a sharp knife to slice each chicken breast in half horizontally to make 8 thin pieces. Place the chicken on a greased baking sheet and cook under a preheated hot broiler for 2 minutes.

- Turn the chicken over and drape a slice of prosciutto over each piece. Return to the broiler for another 2 minutes, until the prosciutto begins to crisp. Place a sage leaf on top of each and cook for another 1 minute, until the chicken is cooked through and the prosciutto and sage are crisp. Serve with green beans and new potatoes.

 ## Prosciutto Roasted Chicken

Use a sharp knife to make a small horizontal slit in the sides of 4 chicken breasts to form a little pocket, making sure you don't cut all the way through the meat. Mix ⅓ cup cream cheese with a handful of chopped basil and the finely grated rind of ½ lemon. Season and stuff a little of the mixture inside each pocket. Smooth over to seal, then wrap a piece of prosciutto around each one. Place on a lightly greased baking sheet and cook in a preheated oven, at 425°F, for 10 minutes. Add 8 cherry tomatoes, drizzle with 1 tablespoon olive oil, and cook for another 5 minutes or until the chicken is cooked through.

Chicken and Bacon Stew

Cut 4 chicken thighs into large chunks. Heat 1 tablespoon vegetable oil in a large skillet and cook the chicken for 5–7 minutes, until golden. Meanwhile, heat 1 tablespoon vegetable oil in a casserole, then add 1 chopped onion and 4 chopped bacon slices. Cook for 5 minutes, until softened. Pour in ½ cup dry white wine and boil until reduced by half. Add the chicken to the casserole along with 2 thyme sprigs and ⅔ cup chicken stock. Simmer for 15 minutes, until the chicken is cooked through. Heat 1 tablespoon oil in the skillet, then add 5 oz sliced wild mushrooms and cook for 3–5 minutes, until soft and lightly browned. Stir the mushrooms into the stew along with 3 tablespoons crème fraîche or sour cream. Serve with mashed potatoes sprinkled with a handful of chopped parsley.

Smoked Duck, Orange, and Watercress Salad

Serves 4

2 large oranges
1 tablespoon rice wine vinegar
3 tablespoons vegetable oil
3 bunches watercress
  or 1 (5 oz) package arugula
1 head of endive
1 scallion, sliced
1¼ cups sliced radishes
8 oz sliced smoked duck breast
salt and black pepper

- Cut the peel from the oranges using a sharp knife. Divide the oranges into segments by cutting between the membranes, holding them over a bowl to catch the juice. Mix the juice with the rice wine vinegar and oil and season well.

- Toss the dressing with the watercress, endive, and scallion. Arrange the salad on serving plates with the orange segments, radishes, and smoked duck.

2 Seared Duck with Citrus Salad

Rub 1 teaspoon five spice powder over 4 duck breasts. Heat a nonstick skillet and cook the duck, skin side down, for 5 minutes. Turn over and cook for another 3–5 minutes, until cooked to your liking. Cut 1 carrot into sticks and cook in a saucepan of lightly salted boiling water with 1½ cups sugar snap peas for 3 minutes or until just cooked through. Drain and cool under cold running water. Whisk together 2 teaspoons finely grated fresh ginger root, 2 teaspoons soy sauce, 3 tablespoons lime juice, 1 tablespoon orange juice, 1 tablespoon honey, and 3 tablespoons vegetable oil. Toss together with the cooked vegetables, 1½ cups shredded napa cabbage, ½ cup bean sprouts, and a large handful of fresh cilantro leaves. Cut the duck into slices and serve alongside the salad.

3 Smoked Duck Risotto with Watercress

Heat 2 tablespoons butter and 1 tablespoon olive oil in a saucepan. Add 1 finely chopped shallot and cook for 5 minutes, until softened. Stir in 1½ cups risotto rice and 1 teaspoon finely grated orange rind, then add ½ cup dry white wine. Cook until simmered away, then gradually stir in 3¾ cups hot chicken stock, a little at a time, stirring frequently, letting the rice absorb the stock before adding more. When the rice is soft, after about 15 minutes, add ⅔ cup frozen peas and 1 cup chopped watercress or 2 cups arugula. Cook until wilted, then add ½ cup grated Parmesan and season to taste. Top with 5 oz sliced smoked duck breast to serve.

20  Mustard Rarebit-Style Pork Chops

Serves 4

4 pork chops
oil, for greasing
½ cup shredded cheddar cheese
2 tablespoons crème fraîche
  or sour cream
1 tablespoon whole-grain
  mustard
salt and black pepper

To serve

green beans
new potatoes

- Put the pork chops on a lightly greased baking sheet, season to taste, and cook in a preheated oven, at 400°F, for 15 minutes.

- Mix together the cheese, crème fraîche, and mustard. Spread a little over the top of each pork chop and return to the oven for 2 minutes or until the topping has just melted. Serve with new potatoes and green beans.

---

1 Creamy Bacon and Mustard Pasta

Heat 1 tablespoon olive oil in a skillet. Cut 6 bacon slices into thin slices, add to the skillet, and cook for 5–7 minutes, until browned and crispy. Cook 1 lb fresh penne pasta in a large saucepan of lightly salted boiling water according to the package directions. Drain and stir in 1 tablespoon whole-grain mustard, the finely grated rind of 1 lemon, and ¼ cup crème fraîche or heavy cream. Add the bacon, season to taste, and sprinkle with chopped parsley to serve.

3 Crispy Mustard Pork Tenderloin

Pat dry 2 pork tenderloins, then dust with all-purpose flour. Brush 2 tablespoons Dijon mustard over the pork and season. Spread 1 cup dry bread crumbs on a plate with a handful of chopped thyme and ½ cup grated Parmesan cheese. Roll the tenderloins in this mixture until well coated. Place on a lightly greased baking sheet and drizzle with 2 tablespoons olive oil. Bake in a preheated oven, at 425°F, for 25 minutes, until golden and cooked through. Serve with baby new potatoes and green vegetables.

Grilled Chorizo with Clam Sauce

Serves 4

4 large cooked chorizo sausages,
   halved lengthwise
3 tablespoons olive oil
1 shallot, finely chopped
1 garlic clove, finely chopped
8 oz clams, scrubbed
⅓ cup water
8 slices ciabatta bread, toasted
8 cherry tomatoes, halved
finely grated rind and juice of
   1 lemon
handful of parsley leaves,
   chopped
arugula leaves, to serve

- Heat a ridged grill pan until smoking. Add the chorizo and cook for 2 minutes on each side or until lightly charred.

- Meanwhile, heat the olive oil in a large saucepan. Add the shallot and garlic and cook for 3 minutes, until softened. Add the clams and the measured water, cover with a lid, and cook for 5 minutes over low heat until the clams have opened, discarding any that do not open.

- Arrange the toasted ciabatta bread and chorizo in serving bowls. Add the tomatoes, lemon rind and juice, and parsley to the pan with the clams and stir until heated through. Spoon the clams over the bread and chorizo and top with arugula leaves.

2 Bacon and Clam Tomato Chowder

Heat 1 tablespoon oil in a large saucepan. Add 1 finely chopped onion and 6 chopped bacon slices. Cook for 5 minutes, until the onion is softened. Add 4 cups vegetable stock, 1 (14½ oz) can diced tomatoes, and 3 chopped potatoes. Simmer for 10 minutes, until the potatoes are beginning to soften, then add 12 oz clams. Cover and cook for 5 minutes, until the clams have opened, discarding any that do not open. Sprinkle with chopped parsley and serve with crusty bread.

3 Pork Meatballs with Clams

Mix together 2 crushed garlic cloves with 1 lb ground pork and ½ cup fresh white bread crumbs and season to taste. Lightly wet your hands and form the mixture into meatballs about the size of a golf ball. Place on a lightly greased baking sheet, drizzle with 1 tablespoon olive oil, and cook in a preheated oven, at 400°F, for 20 minutes. Meanwhile, heat 1 tablespoon olive oil in a large saucepan. Add 1 finely chopped onion and cook for 5 minutes, until softened, add 1 chopped red bell pepper, and stir through 2 teaspoons tomato paste. Pour in ½ cup dry white wine and let simmer reduced by half. Add 1 (14½ oz) can diced tomatoes and 1 teaspoon smoked paprika and season to taste. Let simmer for 5 minutes, then add the meatballs and 8 oz clams. Cover and cook for 5 minutes or until the clams have opened, discarding any that do not open. Sprinkle with chopped parsley before serving.

10 Thai Pork with Mango Salsa

Serves 4

1 lemon grass stalk
2 tablespoons vegetable oil
2 garlic cloves, finely chopped
2 teaspoons chopped fresh
  ginger root
1 pound pork strips
1 teaspoon granulated sugar
2 tablespoons Thai fish sauce
finely grated rind of 1 lime
2 cups cooked rice noodles
4 Boston or other small lettuce,
  leaves separated
handful of fresh cilantro leaves

Salsa

1 mango, peeled, pitted,
  and finely chopped
1 scallion, sliced
1 red chile, finely chopped
juice of 1 lime
salt and black pepper

- Remove the tough outer leaves from the lemon grass and finely shred the core. Heat the oil in a large skillet or wok, add the garlic and lemon grass, and cook for 30 seconds. Stir in the ginger and pork and cook for 5–7 minutes, until the pork is just cooked through. Stir the sugar into the fish sauce to dissolve, add the lime rind, and stir into the pork. Cook for another 1 minute, until glossy and coated.

- Make the salsa by tossing together all the ingredients and seasoning to taste. Mix together the pork, lettuce, and cooked noodles and divide among 4 serving plates. Sprinkle with the fresh cilantro and top with the mango salsa.

---

20 Thai Burgers Coarsely grate 1 small onion, squeeze away the juices, and mix with 1 tablespoon Thai red curry paste, 1 egg yolk, and 1 lb ground pork. Add 1 chopped lemon grass stalk, then form into 4 thick patties. In a smoking hot ridged grill pan, cook the patties for 5–7 minutes on each side, until just cooked through. Make the salsa as above, then stir in some fresh cilantro. Serve the burgers in buns, topped with the salsa.

---

30 Pork Chops with Mango Ginger Chutney Heat 1 tablespoon oil in a saucepan, add ½ teaspoon each coriander and cumin seeds, and cook for 30 seconds, until sizzling. Add 1 finely chopped onion and cook over low heat for 5–7 minutes, until soft and lightly golden. Add 1 cinnamon stick, 2 cardamom pods, and a pinch of ground turmeric. Stir in 2 chopped mangoes, ½ finely chopped red chile, 1 teaspoon finely chopped fresh ginger root, ½ cup white wine vinegar, ½ cup firmly packed light brown sugar, and ½ cup water. Let simmer for 20 minutes, until the mango is soft and the mixture is pulpy. Season to taste. Meanwhile, rub 1 tablespoon oil over 4 pork chops, place under a preheated hot broiler, and cook for 7 minutes on each side, until just cooked through. Serve the chops with a spoonful of the chutney, some green salsa, and rice.

Pork Chops with Plum Ginger Relish

Serves 4

2 tablespoons olive oil
1 small onion, finely chopped
1 tablespoon grated fresh
   ginger root
4 plums, pitted and sliced
1 tablespoon packed light
   brown sugar
1 teaspoon red wine vinegar
finely grated rind of ½ orange
½ cup water
4 pork chops
handful of watercress or arugula,
   to serve
salt and black pepper

- Heat 1 tablespoon oil in a small saucepan, add the onion, and cook for 5 minutes, until softened. Add the ginger, plums, sugar, vinegar, orange rind, and measured water and simmer for 10 minutes, until soft. Season to taste.

- Meanwhile, rub the remaining oil over the chops and season. Cook under a hot broiler for 5 minutes on each side, until just cooked through. Serve with spoonfuls of the relish and some watercress or arugula.

10   Broiled Pork with Plum Salsa

Rub 1 tablespoon oil over 4 pork chops. Season and cook under a hot broiler for 5 minutes on each, side until golden and cooked through. Meanwhile, coarsely chop 3 plums and place in a small bowl. Add 1 finely chopped red chile, the juice of ½ lime, 1 tablespoon orange juice, and 2 tablespoons olive oil. Spoon the salsa over the pork chops to serve.

30   Baked Pork and Plums

Put 4 pork chops in a lightly greased ovenproof dish and arrange 4 halved plums around them. Mix together the juice of 1 orange, 1 teaspoon honey, a pinch of dried red pepper flakes, and 2 teaspoons grated fresh ginger root. Drizzle the mixture over the chops, season, and bake in a preheated oven, at 400°F, for 20 minutes, until browned and the pork is cooked through.

30 Herbed Pork with Creamy Applesauce

Serves 6

2 (1 lb) pork tenderloins
handful of parsley, chopped
2 teaspoons chopped rosemary
10 slices of pancetta
1 tablespoon oil, plus extra
   for greasing
1 onion, chopped
1 apple, cored and cubed
2 tablespoons apple brandy
⅔ cup apple juice
⅓ cup crème fraîche
   or heavy cream
salt and black pepper

To serve

mashed potatoes
watercress or arugula

- Use a sharp knife to slice lengthwise through each tenderloin (being careful not to cut the whole way through) and then open it out like a book.

- Season the meat and sprinkle the herbs over the cut sides, then close them again. Lay half the pancetta slices on a sheet of plastic wrap and place one piece of pork on top. Bring the plastic wrap up and over the pork, so it is wrapped with the pancetta. Repeat with the other tenderloin. Remove the plastic wrap, place on a lightly greased baking sheet, and cook in a preheated oven, at 400°F, for 20–25 minutes, until the meat is cooked through.

- Meanwhile, heat the oil in a skillet. Add the onion and cook for 5 minutes, then stir in the apple and cook over medium heat for another 3 minutes, until softened and browned. Add the brandy to the skillet, let simmer away, then pour in the apple juice. Cook until reduced by half. Stir in the crème fraîche and season to taste.

- Cut the pork into thick slices and spoon the sauce over the top. Serve with mashed potatoes and watercress.

---

1 Bacon and Apple Salad

Cook 6 bacon slices under a hot broiler for 3 minutes on each side, until just crisp, then cut into slices. Whisk together 1 tablespoon white wine vinegar, 1 teaspoon Dijon mustard, and 3 tablespoons olive oil and season. Thinly slice 2 apples and toss with the dressing and 7 cups mixed salad greens. Stir through the bacon and serve.

2 Crispy Pork Chops with Apple Slaw

Lay 6 trimmed pork chops between sheets of plastic wrap and flatten with a meat mallet or rolling pin until ½ inch thick. Pour 1 extra-large beaten egg onto a plate. Mix together 1½ cups dry bread crumbs with ½ cup grated Parmesan on a plate. Dip the pork into the egg, then the bread crumbs to coat. Heat 3 tablespoons oil in a nonstick skillet and cook the pork for 5–7 minutes on each side, until golden and crisp. Meanwhile, finely shred ½ cabbage. Mix the cabbage with 1 apple, cut into matchsticks. Stir 1 teaspoon white wine vinegar together with ½ cup each of mayonnaise and plain yogurt and season. Toss with the apple and cabbage and serve with the pork.

 # Pork and Pineapple Curry

Serves 4

1¾ cups canned coconut milk
2 tablespoons Thai red
  curry paste
2 teaspoons packed light
  brown sugar
2 tablespoons Thai fish sauce
2 tablespoons tamarind paste
2 lime leaves
1 tablespoon oil
12 oz pork, cubed
1 (8 oz) can pineapple chunks
handful of fresh cilantro, chopped
½ cup bean sprouts
rice, to serve

- Heat a large saucepan. Scoop the thick coconut cream from the top of the can, add it to a saucepan with the curry paste, and cook over medium heat for 2–3 minutes, until really fragrant. Add the remaining coconut milk, the sugar, fish sauce, tamarind paste, and lime leaves and simmer for 5 minutes.

- Meanwhile, heat a large skillet and add the oil. Add the pork and cook for 5 minutes, until browned all over. Add the pork to the curry, stir in the pineapple, and cook for another 10 minutes. Sprinkle with the cilantro and bean sprouts and serve with plain rice.

 Ham with Fresh Pineapple Sauce

Rub 1 tablespoon oil over 4 cooked ham steaks and cook under a preheated hot broiler for 2–3 minutes on each side, until lightly browned. Mix 1 (8 oz) can pineapple chunks with 1 tablespoon finely chopped red onion, ½ finely chopped green chile, a large handful of chopped fresh cilantro, and ⅓ cup pineapple juice and season. Spoon the sauce over the ham to serve.

Pork and Pineapple Wraps

Use a mandolin to cut ½ peeled pineapple into very thin circles. Set aside. Heat 1 tablespoon oil in a skillet, add 12 oz ground pork, and cook over hight heat for 7 minutes, until starting to brown. Add 2 crushed garlic cloves, 1 teaspoon finely grated fresh ginger root, ½ seeded and finely chopped red chile, and 1 finely chopped lemon grass stalk and cook for 1 minute. Pour in 2 tablespoons Thai fish sauce and ⅓ cup pineapple juice and let cook until simmered away. Stir through a handful of chopped fresh cilantro. Separate the leaves of a Boston or other small lettuce. Put a heaping spoonful of pork on each pineapple slice, place on a lettuce leaf with some cilantro leaves, roll up, and serve.

Roasted Sausages with Polenta

Serves 4

1 tablespoon olive oil
8 sausages
8 cherry tomatoes
½ cup fresh red pepper pesto
¼ cup water
5 cups vegetable stock
2 cups instant polenta or cornmeal
½ cup mascarpone
salt

- Toss together the oil and sausages in a roasting pan and cook in a preheated oven, at 400°F, for 12 minutes. Give the pan good shake, add the tomatoes, and cook for another 7 minutes, until the sausages are browned and the tomatoes are starting to wilt. Remove from the pan and keep warm.

- Add the pesto to the pan with the measured water and stir together until warm.

- Meanwhile, heat the stock in a large saucepan with salt to taste. Add the polenta and simmer for 5 minutes, stirring frequently, until thickened like mashed potatoes. Stir the mascarpone through the polenta.

- Spoon the polenta onto serving plates. Top with the sausages and tomatoes and drizzle with the pesto.

Grilled Chorizo and Polenta

Cut 1 lb of a cooked polenta log into thick strips. Brush with 1 tablespoon olive oil and cook in a preheated, ridged grill pan for 2 minutes on each side, until lightly charred. Keep warm. Slice 5 oz chorizo and grill for 1 minute on each side, until browned. Toss 8 halved cherry tomatoes and 1 (5 oz) package arugula leaves with 1 tablespoon balsamic vinegar and 3 tablespoons extra virgin olive oil and season to taste. Serve the salad with the chorizo and polenta.

Bacon Corn Muffins

Cook 4 bacon slices under a preheated hot broiler for 5 minutes, until just cooked through, and chop into small pieces. Meanwhile, place 1¼ cups all-purpose flour, 1 cup cornmeal, 2 teaspoons baking powder, 2 eggs, 6 tablespoons melted butter, and 1¼ cups buttermilk in a food processor and blend together until smooth. Season to taste. Add 1 cup corn kernels and stir into the batter with the bacon. Spoon into a well-greased 12-cup muffin pan and cook in a preheated oven, at 400°F, for 20–25 minutes or until just cooked through. Serve with sliced tomatoes and a green salad.

Broiled Lamb with Minted Peas

Serves 4

2 tablespoons olive oil
1 onion, finely chopped
1 garlic clove, crushed
1 cup chicken stock
3⅓ cups frozen peas
handful of mint leaves, chopped
2 (10 oz) lamb cutlets
⅓ cup crumbled feta cheese
salt and black pepper

- Heat 1 tablespoon oil in a saucepan, add the onion, and cook for 5 minutes, until softened. Stir in the garlic and cook for another 1 minute. Add the stock and simmer for 2–3 minutes, then add the peas and cook for 3 minutes, until soft. Reserve some of the peas, then blend the remainder with an immersion blender until nearly smooth. Stir in most of the mint and season to taste.

- Rub the remaining oil over the lamb and season well. Cook under a hot broiler for 5-7 minutes on each side, until browned and just cooked through.

- Slice the lamb and arrange on serving plates with the mashed peas. Sprinkle with the reserved peas, remaining mint, and feta to serve.

Lamb with Pea Salad

Rub 2 teaspoons oil over 8 small lamb chops. Cook under a hot broiler for 3–5 minutes on each side, until golden and charred. Meanwhile, cook 1 cup frozen peas in lightly salted boiling water for 3 minutes, until soft. Drain and cool under cold running water. Whisk together 3 tablespoons olive oil with a good squeeze of lemon juice and season to taste. Toss with 4 cups pea shoots, a handful of chopped mint, 1 sliced scallion, and the cooled peas. Sprinkle with ⅓ cup crumbled feta cheese and serve with the chops.

Spring Lamb Stew

Heat 1 tablespoon oil in a saucepan, add 1 chopped onion, and cook for 5 minutes, until softened. Halve 3 small carrots and add to the pan with 1 lb new potatoes. Pour in 1½ cups vegetable stock. Bring to a boil and simmer for 15–20 minutes, until the vegetables are soft. Add 1 cup frozen peas and cook for another 3 minutes, until soft. Meanwhile, rub 1 tablespoon oil over 2 lamb sirloin chops. Cook under a hot broiler for 5 minutes on each side, until golden and cooked through, then cut into thick slices. Stir some chopped parsley and mint through the stew and top with the lamb.

30 Rack of Lamb with Harissa Dressing

Serves 4–6

1 cup hazelnuts
½ cup sesame seeds
2 tablespoons coriander seeds
1 tablespoon cumin seeds
¼ cup olive oil
2 racks of lamb
2 red bell peppers, cored,
  seeded, and thickly sliced
2 tablespoons harissa
⅓ cup plain yogurt
salt and black pepper
couscous, to serve

- Put the nuts and spices in a small, dry skillet and cook for 1 minute. Transfer to a mortar and crush coarsely with a pestle, adding a little salt.

- Rub 2 tablespoons oil over the lamb racks, season well, and press the nut mixture onto the fatty side of each rack. Transfer to a shallow roasting pan and bake in a preheated oven, at 425°F, for 10 minutes. Arrange the bell peppers around the lamb and cook for another 10–15 minutes for rare to medium lamb.

- Swirl the harissa over the yogurt in a bowl. Slice the lamb racks and serve with the bell peppers, drizzling with the harissa sauce before serving with couscous.

10 Harissa Lamb Wraps

Mix 1 tablespoon lemon juice and the finely grated rind of ½ lemon with 1 tablespoon harissa and 1 tablespoon olive oil. Season to taste and toss with 12 oz diced leg of lamb. Heat a ridged grill pan until smoking and cook the lamb together with 1 sliced onion for 3 minutes on each side, until charred and cooked through. Heat 4 large flatbreads on the ridged grill pan for 30 seconds, then arrange the onions and lamb on top. Place ¼ cucumber, cut into chunks, and 2 cups shredded lettuce on top and drizzle with some plain yogurt, then wrap and serve.

20 Easy Spiced Lamb Pilaf

Heat 1 tablespoon olive oil in a casserole, add 1 tablespoon harissa, then add 12 oz diced leg of lamb. Stir around the dish until well coated, then stir in 1½ cups basmati or other long-grain rice. Pour in 2½ cups chicken stock and bring to a boil. Let simmer, uncovered, for 10 minutes. Stir in 1 (5 oz) package baby spinach leaves, reduce the heat to low, cover, and cook for another 5 minutes, until the rice is soft. Sprinkle with mint leaves and drizzle with yogurt to serve.

Lamb Cutlets with Tomatoes, Feta, and Mashed Chickpeas

Serves 4

¼ cup olive oil

1 onion, chopped

2 garlic cloves, crushed

½ teaspoon ground cumin

2 (15 oz) cans chickpeas, rinsed and drained

⅓ cup chicken stock or water

2 tablespoons lemon juice

4 lamb cutlets

4 cherry tomatoes, halved

⅓ cup crumbled feta cheese

handful of oregano, chopped

salt and black pepper

- Heat 2 tablespoons oil in a saucepan, add the onion, and cook for 5 minutes, until softened. Stir in the garlic and cumin and cook for a few seconds. Add the chickpeas, then pour in the stock or water and let simmer for 2–3 minutes, until warm through. Season to taste. Use an immersion blender or transfer to a food processor and blend to make a coarse puree. Squeeze the lemon juice over the top and keep warm.

- Rub 1 tablespoon oil over the lamb, season, and cook under a preheated hot broiler for 5–7 minutes on each side, until golden and just cooked through.

- Pile the tomatoes, cheese, and oregano on top of the lamb. Drizzle with the remaining oil and cook under the hot broiler for another 1–2 minutes, until golden. Serve with the mashed chickpea.

---

10 **Lamb Burgers with Tomato Feta Salsa**

Rub 1 tablespoon oil over 4 prepared lamb patties. Cook in a preheated ridged grill pan for 4 minutes on each side, until cooked through. Meanwhile, toss together 8 halved cherry tomatoes, 2 teaspoons red wine vinegar, 3 tablespoons olive oil, 1 crushed garlic clove, ⅓ cup feta cheese, and a handful of oregano. Season to taste and put the burgers in buns and top with the salsa and a handful of arugula leaves.

30 **Lamb, Feta, and Tomato Gratin**

Heat 1 tablespoon olive oil in a large, ovenproof skillet, add 1 chopped onion, and cook for 5 minutes, until softened. Stir in 1 lb ground lamb and cook for another 5 minutes, breaking up any clumps. Add 2 crushed garlic cloves and 2 teaspoons tomato paste and cook for another 30 seconds. Pour in 1 (14½ oz) can diced tomatoes and a splash of water. Add a handful of chopped oregano, season to taste, and simmer for 10–15 minutes. Sprinkle with ½ cup crumbled feta cheese, cook under a preheated hot broiler for 1 minute and then serve.

20 Baked Lamb and Red Peppers with Mint Salsa

Serves 4

8 lamb loin chops

2 red bell peppers, cored, seeded, and cut into wedges

5 unpeeled garlic cloves

¼ cup olive oil

juice and finely grated rind of ½ lemon

pinch of granulated sugar

½ teaspoon Dijon mustard

large handful of basil leaves, minced

large handful of mint leaves, minced

salt and black pepper

- Arrange the lamb, bell peppers, and garlic on a baking sheet. Drizzle with 1 tablespoon oil, season well, and bake in a preheated oven, at 400°F, for 15–20 minutes, until lightly browned and just cooked through.

- Whisk together the lemon rind and juice, the sugar, and mustard and the remaining oil. Season to taste and stir through the herbs. Drizzle the dressing over the lamb and bell peppers and serve with new potatoes.

---

10 Lamb and Red Pepper Kebabs

Core, seed, and cut 1 red bell pepper into squares. Thread the pepper onto barbecue skewers, alternating with 1 lb lamb chunks. Drizzle with 1 tablespoon vegetable oil, season, and cook on a smoking ridged grill pan for 3 minutes on each side, until charred and just cooked through. Sprinkle with the finely grated rind of 1 lemon and a handful of chopped mint leaves before serving.

30 Lamb Burgers with Red Pepper Tomato Relish

Core, seed, and thickly slice 2 red bell peppers. Heat 2 tablespoons olive oil in a saucepan, add the bell peppers, and cook for 10 minutes. Add 8 halved cherry tomatoes, a pinch of dried red pepper flakes, and cook for another 10 minutes. Stir in 1 teaspoon white wine vinegar and 1 teaspoon granulated sugar, season to taste, and cook for another 2–3 minutes, until thick and pulpy. Meanwhile, mix together 1 lb ground lamb, 1 crushed garlic clove, a pinch of dried red pepper flakes, a handful of mint leaves, and 1 egg yolk. Form the mixture into 4 patties, brush with 2 teaspoons olive oil, and season. Cook in a hot ridged grill pan for 5–7 minutes on each side, until cooked through. Place in buns or pita breads, top with the relish and a handful arugula, and serve.

Individual Beef Wellingtons

Serves 4

4 thick tenderloin steaks
⅓ cup mushroom pâté
4 slices of prosciutto
2 sheets ready-to-bake
  puff pastry
1 egg, beaten
oil, for greasing
4 thyme sprigs
salt and black pepper

To serve

sugar snap peas
roasted new potatoes

- Place a heaping tablespoon of pâté on each steak and then wrap in a slice of prosciutto.

- Cut each pastry sheet into 2 squares and brush with a little egg. Place a steak in the center of each, fold over the corners of the pastry, and tuck together to seal.

- Place the pastry packages, seal side down, on a lightly greased baking sheet, brush the tops with a little more egg, and top with a sprig of thyme. Bake in a preheated oven, at 425°F, for 12–15 minutes, until the pastry is puffed and golden. Serve with sugar snap peas and roasted new potatoes.

---

10 Beef and Mushroom Melts

Heat 1 tablespoon oil in a skillet and sauté 1 sliced onion for about 7 minutes, until soft and golden. In another skillet, cook 1 cup sliced mushrooms for 3–5 minutes, until soft. Pile the onion and mushrooms onto one half of 4 split rolls. Top with 5 oz sliced roasted beef and 4 slices of cheddar cheese. Place under a hot broiler until the cheese starts to melt, then add the tops of the rolls and serve.

20 Steaks with Mushroom Sauce

Heat a skillet until it is smoking and then add 1 tablespoon oil and 1 tablespoon butter to the skillet. Add 1 sliced onion and cook for 5–7 minutes, until softened. Add 2 cups sliced mushrooms and cook for another 2 minutes, until softened. Add 1 crushed garlic clove and cook for 30 seconds. Carefully pour in 2 tablespoons brandy and simmer until reduced. Add ⅓ cup crème fraîche or heavy cream and cook until thickened. Keep the sauce warm. Rub 1 tablespoon oil over 4 tenderloin steaks and season. Cook on a smoking ridged grill pan for 2–3 minutes on each side, until browned but still pink inside. Set the beef aside to rest, then spoon the sauce over the steaks just before serving.

Vietnamese Beef Skewers

Serves 4

2 lemon grass stalks
1 garlic clove, crushed
1 red chile
1 small shallot
3 teaspoons light brown sugar
¼ cup Thai fish sauce
1 lb steak strips
1 tablespoon oil
1¼ lb fresh rice noodles
squeeze of lime juice
¼ iceberg lettuce, shredded
2 carrots, grated
handful of mint leaves

- Put the lemon grass, garlic, chile, shallot, half the sugar, and 2 tablespoons fish sauce in a blender and blend to form a chunky paste.

- Rub the mixture all over the beef and thread the meat onto skewers. Drizzle with the oil. Heat a large, ridged grill pan until smoking, then cook the skewers for 1–2 minutes on each side, until charred.

- Meanwhile, cook the noodles according to the package directions, cool under cold running water, and drain. Stir together the remaining sugar and fish sauce with the lime juice. Toss through the noodles along with the lettuce, carrots, and mint leaves and serve with the skewers.

2 Stir-Fried Rice with Beef

In a smoking ridged grill pan, cook 2 large steaks for 2–3 minutes on each side, until charred but still pink in the middle, then set aside to rest. Boil 1¼ cups rice according to the package directions until soft, then drain. Heat 1 tablespoon oil in a wok, add 1 chopped shallot, and cook for 2 minutes. Add 1 finely chopped garlic clove, 2 teaspoons grated fresh ginger root, 1 finely chopped lemon grass stalk, and ½ chopped red chile and cook for 1 minute. Add 1 sliced red bell pepper and cook for 2 minutes. Stir in the rice and 2 tablespoons Thai fish sauce. Slice the beef and add to the pan with some chopped basil to serve.

3 Braised Vietnamese Beef

Heat 2 tablespoons oil in a saucepan, add 1 sliced onion, and cook for 5 minutes, until softened. Add 2 crushed garlic cloves, 2 teaspoons finely grated fresh ginger root, 1 finely chopped lemon grass stalk, and 1 seeded and chopped red chile. Stir around the pan for 1 minute. Pour in 1¼ cups beef stock, 3 tablespoons Thai fish sauce, and 1 tablespoon packed light brown sugar. Bring to a boil and let simmer for 15 minutes. Rub 1 tablespoon oil over 4 steaks. Heat a ridged grill pan until smoking, season the steaks, and cook for 2–3 minutes on each side, until charred but still pink in the middle. Cut the meat into thick pieces and add to the braise for 2 minutes to heat through. Serve over plain rice.

FOO-MEAT-FAO

Steak with Blue Cheese Butter and Scallion Mashed Potatoes

Serves 4

7 potatoes (1¾ lb), peeled
  and quartered
½ cup crème fraîche
  or sour cream
2 scallions, sliced
4 tablespoons butter, softened
1 garlic clove, crushed
8 oz blue cheese
¼ cup finely chopped toasted
  walnuts
handful of parsley, chopped
1 tablespoon olive oil
4 rib-eye steaks
salt and black pepper

- Cook the potatoes in a large saucepan of lightly salted boiling water for 12–15 minutes, until soft. Mash until smooth. Reserve ¼ cup crème fraîche and stir the remaining ¼ cup into the potatoes along with the scallions, season to taste, and keep warm.

- Meanwhile, stir together the butter, garlic, and blue cheese, then add the walnuts and parsley and season to taste. Place in a sheet of plastic wrap and roll up to form a cylinder. Twist the ends to seal and place in the freezer for 5–10 minutes, until firm.

- Heat a ridged grill pan until smoking. Rub the oil over the steaks and season well. Cook for 2–3 minutes on each side for medium rare. Let rest for a minute or two, then place on serving plates with the mashed potatoes and top with a slice of the flavored butter.

---

10 Beef Salad with Blue Cheese Dressing Whisk together ⅓ cup olive oil with 2 tablespoons white wine vinegar, crumble in 2 oz blue cheese, and stir until smooth. Heat a ridged grill pan until smoking. Rub 1 tablespoon oil over 8 thin steaks and season. Cook for 1–2 minutes on each side, until seared but still just pink in the middle. Toss the dressing with 1 (7 oz) package mixed salad greens and 2 cups croutons, then add 8 halved cherry tomatoes and 2 sliced scallions. Serve with the steaks.

---

30 Steak with Blue Cheese Sauce and Onion Rings Heat 2 tablespoons butter in a saucepan, add 1 chopped shallot, and cook for 3 minutes. Stir in 1 crushed garlic clove and cook for 1 minute more. Crumble in 8 oz blue cheese and whisk until melted, then stir in ⅓ cup crème fraîche or sour cream and a handful of chopped chives. Keep warm. Slice 3 onions into thick rings, put them in a bowl with 2 cups buttermilk, and stir until well covered. Place 1⅔ cups flour into a bowl with some salt and a pinch of cayenne. Heat a large saucepan one-third full with oil until hot enough that a cube of bread dropped into the oil will sizzle and brown in 15 seconds. Working in batches, remove some onion rings from the buttermilk and dip into the flour until well coated. Shake off any excess flour and cook the onion in the hot oil for 2–3 minutes, until golden. Keep warm in the oven. Cook 4 rib-eye steaks as above. Serve with the sauce drizzled over the top, along with the onion rings and some lightly steamed spinach.

Porcini Meatballs

Serves 6

1 oz dried porcini mushrooms

½ cup boiling water

1½ cups fresh white bread crumbs

¼ cup milk

1¼ lb ground beef

1 egg, beaten

¼ cup grated Parmesan cheese, plus extra to serve

1 rosemary sprig, finely chopped

1 garlic clove, crushed

2 tablespoons olive oil

2 cups prepared fresh tomato sauce

1¼ lb spaghetti

salt and black pepper

- Put the mushrooms in a small saucepan, cover with the measured boiling water, and simmer for 2 minutes, until soft. Drain, reserving the liquid.

- Meanwhile, put the bread crumbs in a small bowl, pour the milk over them, and let sit for 1–2 minutes, until absorbed, then mix together with the beef, egg, Parmesan, rosemary, and garlic. Finely chop the porcini and stir into the mixture. Season to taste. Lightly wet your hands and form the mixture into meatballs about the size of a walnut.

- Heat the oil in a large skillet, add the meatballs, and cook for 5–7 minutes, turning occasionally, until golden all over. Strain the mushroom soaking liquid, discarding any grit, and add to the pan with the tomato sauce. Let simmer for 15 minutes or until the meatballs are cooked through.

- Meanwhile, cook the spaghetti according to the package directions. Drain, reserving a little of the cooking water, and return to the pan. Add the meatballs to the pan, together with some of the cooking water to loosen, if needed. Transfer to serving bowls and sprinkle with Parmesan shavings.

---

1 Mushroom and Beef Salad

Toss 8 oz mushrooms with 3 tablespoons olive oil and season to taste. Broil or grill for 3–5 minutes, until softened and lightly charred. Whisk together ⅓ cup olive oil with 3 tablespoons lemon juice and season. Toss the dressing with 1½ (5 oz) packages arugula leaves. Arrange on a plate with 1 lb sliced rare roast beef and the mushrooms. Top with Parmesan cheese shavings.

2 Steak with Creamy Mushroom and Tomato Sauce

Heat 2 tablespoons olive oil in a skillet, add 8 oz wild mushrooms, and cook for 3 minutes, until golden. Add 1 chopped garlic clove and cook for another 30 seconds. Add 1 teaspoon tomato paste and ½ cup dry white wine. Let simmer for 2 minutes, until reduced, then stir through ⅓ cup crème fraîche or heavy cream followed by 8 halved cherry tomatoes. Season to taste and let simmer for 2 minutes or until the tomatoes have softened. Meanwhile, rub 3 tablespoons oil over 6 steaks and season well. Heat a ridged grill pan until smoking and cook the steaks for 2–3 minutes on each side. Cook 1¼ lb egg noodles according to the package directions, drain, and toss through 2 tablespoons butter. Serve alongside the steaks with the sauce spooned over them.

30 Seared Beef Tenderloin with Horseradish Sauce and Tomatoes

Serves 4

1½ lb new potatoes, halved

¼ cup olive oil

4 small plum tomatoes, halved

2 teaspoons balsamic vinegar

1 teaspoon granulated sugar

1½ lb beef tenderloin

2–3 tablespoons horseradish
  sauce

½ cup crème fraîche
  or sour cream

salt and black pepper

- Toss the potatoes with 2 tablespoons oil, season, and place on a baking sheet. Cook in a preheated oven, at 400°F, for 20 minutes. Put the tomatoes, cut side up, on the baking sheet, drizzle with 1 tablespoon olive oil, then sprinkle with the vinegar and sugar. Cook for another 5 minutes, until the potatoes are soft and the tomatoes are lightly charred.

- Meanwhile, heat a large, ovenproof skillet until smoking. Season the beef well, then swirl the remaining oil around the skillet and add the beef. Cook for 1 minute on each side, until browned all over, then transfer the skillet to the oven and cook for 12–15 minutes for medium rare. Let the beef rest for a couple of minutes, then cut into thick slices.

- Stir together the horseradish sauce and crème fraîche. Arrange the beef on a plate along with the tomatoes and potatoes. Serve with the horseradish sauce.

10 Roast Beef Salad with Horseradish Dressing

Cook 1 cup green beans in boiling water for 3–5 minutes, until just soft. Drain and cool under cold running water. Toss the beans with 1 (5 oz) package arugula, 2 diced tomatoes, 3 tablespoons olive oil, and 1 tablespoon lemon juice. Arrange on a platter with 8 oz sliced roast beef. Mix 3 tablespoons horseradish sauce with ⅓ cup sour cream, 2 tablespoons milk, and a handful of chopped chives. Drizzle the dressing over the salad to serve.

20 Seared Steak with Horseradish Mashed Poatoes

Cook 7 peeled and quartered potatoes (1¾ lb) in a large saucepan of boiling water for 12–15 minutes, until soft. Mash and stir in ½ cup crème fraîche or sour cream and 1–2 tablespoons horseradish sauce. Meanwhile, heat a large skillet until smoking. Swirl 1 tablespoon oil around the skillet. Season 4 tenderloin steaks really well, add to the skillet, and cook for 2–3 minutes on each side for medium rare.

Whisk 1 tablespoon balsamic vinegar with 3 tablespoons olive oil and season. Toss together with 1 bunch watercress leaves or 1 (5 oz) package arugula and 8 halved cherry tomatoes. Serve with the steaks and mashed potatoes.

Beef Strips with Tomato, Paprika, and Caramelized Onion

Serves 4

2 tablespoons vegetable oil
1 onion, sliced
2 garlic cloves, crushed
2 teaspoons tomato paste
1 teaspoon granulated sugar
1 teaspoon smoked paprika
8 cherry tomatoes
3 large tenderloin steaks
3 tablespoons brandy
½ cup sour cream
salt and black pepper
plain boiled rice, to serve

- Heat 1 tablespoon oil in a large skillet and cook the onion over low heat for 15 minutes, until really soft. Stir in the garlic, tomato paste, sugar, and paprika and cook for another 1 minute. Add the cherry tomatoes and cook for 2 minutes or until starting to wilt. Carefully add the brandy to the skillet and cook for 1 minute, until reduced down.

- Meanwhile, heat the remaining oil in another large skillet, add the steaks, and cook for 3 minutes on each side, until golden but still pink in the middle. Set aside for a couple of minutes to rest.

- Cut the steak into thick strips and arrange on serving plates, then spoon the tomato sauce and sour cream them. Serve with plain rice.

Creamy Beef and Tomato Toasts

Lightly toast 4 large pieces of sourdough bread. Toss 8 cherry tomatoes with 1 tablespoon olive oil and 1 crushed garlic clove in a roasting pan, season to taste, and cook under a preheated hot broiler for 2 minutes, until the tomatoes start to burst. Arrange 5 oz sliced roasted beef on the bread and spoon the tomato mixture over the top. Then spoon 1 tablespoon sour cream over each toast and top with a sprinkling of paprika and some arugula to serve.

Creamy Tomato and Beef Pasta Gratin Heat 1 tablespoon oil in a large skillet, then add 1 lb ground beef and cook for 5 minutes or until browned. Add 2 finely chopped garlic cloves and 1 teaspoon each tomato paste and paprika and cook for another 1 minute. Pour in 1 (14½ oz) can diced tomatoes and simmer for 10 minutes, then stir in 2 tablespoons crème fraîche or heavy cream. Meanwhile, cook 12 oz penne according to the package directions. Drain and mix with 1 cup crème fraîche or heavy cream and 2 tablespoons water to loosen the mixture. Spoon the beef into an ovenproof dish, top with the pasta, and sprinkle with ¾ cup shredded mozzarella cheese and a handful of grated Parmesan. Cook under a hot broiler for 3–5 minutes, until golden.

QuickCook
Fish

Recipes listed by cooking time

30

20

Seared Shrimp with Squid Ink Pasta

Serves 4

1 lb squid ink spaghetti
⅓ cup olive oil
3 garlic cloves, finely chopped
1–2 red chiles, seeded and
  chopped
8 oz large, raw peeled shrimp
⅓ cup dry white wine
handful of parsley, finely chopped
salt

- Cook the pasta in a large saucepan of lightly salted boiling water according to the package directions.

- Meanwhile, heat the oil in a large skillet, add the garlic and chiles, and cook for 30 seconds. Add the shrimp and cook for 1–2 minutes on each side, until turning golden. Add the wine and cook until nearly boiled away.

- Drain the pasta, reserving a little of the cooking water. Add the shrimp and juices to the skillet, along with a little cooking water to loosen it, if necessary. Stir through the parsley and serve.

20 Salt and Pepper Shrimp with Squid

Squid Stir ⅔ cup cornstarch, 2 teaspoons sea salt flakes, ½ teaspoon black pepper, and a pinch each of Chinese five spice powder and cayenne pepper with ¼ cup ice cold water. Toss 8 oz large, raw peeled shrimp with 8 oz squid, cut into rings, in the cornstarch mixture. Heat a large saucepan one-third full of oil until it is hot enough that a piece of bread will sizzle in 15 seconds. Cook the shrimp and squid, in batches, for 1–2 minutes, until golden and crisp. Drain on paper towels and serve with lemon wedges and a green salad.

30 Squid Ink and Shrimp Paella

Heat 2½ cups fish or chicken stock in a saucepan with 1 teaspoon squid ink. Heat a large saucepan, add 2 tablespoons olive oil, and stir in 5 oz sliced chorizo. Cook for 1 minute. Add 1 finely chopped onion and cook for another 5 minutes, until softened, then add 2 finely chopped garlic cloves and 1 finely chopped red chile. Cook for 30 seconds and add 1½ cups paella or risotto rice. Stir around the pan until well coated. Pour the stock into the rice pan and let cook, uncovered, for 10 minutes. Put 5 oz large, raw peeled shrimp on top with 8 halved cherry tomatoes. Cover and cook for another 5 minutes over low heat. Stir through 5 oz squid rings, heat for 30 seconds, then squeeze over some lemon juice, sprinkle with chopped parsley, and serve.

Sea Bream in a Salt Fennel Crust with Lemon Dressing

Serves 4

9 cups kosher salt (4 lb)
1 tablespoon fennel seeds
2 egg whites, lightly beaten
2 sea bream, scaled and gutted
1 lemon
1 lime
1 orange
½ fennel bulb, thinly sliced
¼ cup extra virgin olive oil
handful of chives, chopped
salt and black pepper

· Mix together the salt and fennel seeds and stir through the egg whites. Spread about one-third of this mixture over the bottom of a large ovenproof dish. Place the fish on top, then cover with the remaining salt, making sure you don't have any gaps, although it's fine for the tails to be showing. Bake in a preheated oven, at 400°F, for 20 minutes.

· Meanwhile, cut the peel from the citrus fruits using a sharp knife. Divide the fruits into segments by cutting between the membranes, holding them over a bowl to catch the juice. Place in the bowl with the juice and the remaining ingredients and season.

· To serve, crack open the salt crust by giving it a sharp tap with the back of a heavy knife. Peel away the salt crust, remove the fish fillets, and serve with the dressing alongside.

 Grilled Sea Bream with Fennel

Salsa Verde Rub 1 tablespoon olive oil over 4 sea bream fillets and season well. Cook on a smoking ridged grill pan, skin side down, for 5 minutes, then turn over and cook for another 3 minutes, until charred and just cooked through. Meanwhile, finely chop ¼ fennel bulb. Mix together with 3 tablespoons olive oil, the finely grated rind of 1 lemon and 1 tablespoon lemon juice, 2 teaspoons capers, and a handful of chopped parsley. Spoon it over the fish to serve.

Sea Bream Baked on Salt

Spread 4½ cups kosher salt (2 lb) over a baking sheet. Thinly slice 1 fennel bulb and place on top of the salt together with some thyme sprigs. Lay 4 sea bream fillets on top, skin side up, and bake in a preheated oven, at 400°F, for 10–12 minutes, until the fish just starts to flake. Carefully lift off the salt, squeeze a little lemon juice over the top, and serve.

20 Broiled Swordfish with Warm Romesco Salad

Serves 4

⅓ cup olive oil

2 red bell peppers, cored, seeded, and quartered

2 slices of ciabatta bread, torn into chunks

1 garlic clove, crushed

1 tablespoon sherry vinegar

½ teaspoon smoked paprika

1 tomato, cut into wedges

4 swordfish steaks

¼ cup blanched almonds

¼ cup blanched hazelnuts

handful of parsley, chopped

salt and black pepper

- Rub 1 tablespoon oil over the bell peppers, season, and cook under a hot broiler for 5–8 minutes, until charred all over. Toss the bread in another tablespoon of oil and broil for 3 minutes, turn ove,r and cook for another 2 minutes, until just crisp and golden. Set aside.

- Whisk together the garlic, vinegar, smoked paprika, and 3 tablespoons olive oil to form a dressing, and toss together with the warm bell peppers and the tomatoes. Set aside.

- Rub 1 tablespoon olive oil over the swordfish steaks, season, and cook under a preheated hot broiler for 5 minutes on each side, until golden and just cooked through.

- Meanwhile, heat a dry skillet and cook the nuts for 2 minutes, until lightly browned, then coarsely chop. Toss the bell pepper mixture with the bread and most of the nuts and parsley. Serve alongside the fish with some more parsley and nuts sprinkled over the top.

10 Grilled Swordfish with Romesco Dip

In a small food processor, blend together 1 roasted red pepper with ¼ cup toasted slivered almonds, ½ slice of white bread, 3 plum tomatoes, 1 tablespoon sherry vinegar, ½ teaspoon smoked paprika, and 3 tablespoons olive oil to make a smooth sauce. Season. Rub 1 tablespoon olive oil over 4 swordfish steaks and season well. Cook on a ridged grill pan for 5 minutes on each side or until just cooked through. Serve with the dipping sauce and a salad.

30 Swordfish and Romesco Stew

Heat 2 tablespoons olive oil in a large saucepan, add 1 finely chopped onion, and cook for 5 minutes, until softened. Add 1 finely chopped fennel bulb and cook for another 5 minutes. Stir in 2 crushed garlic cloves, a pinch of dried red pepper flakes, and ½ teaspoon smoked paprika. Add 1 tablespoon sherry vinegar and ½ cup dry white wine and let simmer away. Add 1 (14½ oz) can diced tomatoes and simmer for another 10 minutes. Meanwhile, grind ¼ cup toasted slivered almonds in a small food processor. Stir into the stew along with 2 chopped roasted red peppers and simmer for a few minutes. Then add 4 swordfish steaks and let cook for 5–7 minutes, until just cooked through. Sprinkle with a handful of chopped parsley and serve with toasted ciabatta bread.

Manhattan Clam Chowder

Serves 4

1 lb clams, scrubbed
½ cup dry white wine
1 tablespoon oil
4 oz bacon, chopped
1 large onion, chopped
1 celery stick, chopped
1 carrot, peeled and chopped
3 potatoes, peeled and chopped
1 (14½ oz) can diced tomatoes
1 thyme sprig
6 cups fish stock
salt and black pepper
crusty bread or crackers, to serve

- Put the clams in a large saucepan with the wine, cover, and cook for 5 minutes or until the clams have opened. Discard any that do not open. Remove the clam meat from most of the shells, keeping some in their shells for decoration, and reserve the juice.

- Meanwhile, heat the oil in a large saucepan, add the bacon, and cook for 2 minutes, until browned. Stir in the onion, celery, and carrot and cook for another 5 minutes, until softened. Then add the potatoes, tomatoes, thyme, stock, and the cooking liquid from the clams.

- Cook for 12–15 minutes, until the potatoes are soft. Season and return the clam meat and whole clams to the pan. Heat through and serve with crusty bread or crackers.

Clam and Tomato Linguine

Heat 1 tablespoon olive oil in a large saucepan, add 2 crushed garlic cloves, and cook for 30 seconds. Add ½ cup dry white wine and add 1 lb scrubbed clams. Cover and cook for 5 minutes, until the clams have opened. Discard any that do not open. Stir in 1 tablespoon lemon juice and 8 halved cherry tomatoes. Cook 1 lb fresh linguine according to the package directions, drain, reserving a little cooking water, then stir in the clams with 2 tablespoons butter and some cooking water, if needed. Sprinkle with chopped parsley and serve.

Clam and Spicy Tomato Pizza

Mix 2 (6½ oz) packages pizza crust mix according to the package directions and knead for 3 minutes. Divide the dough into 4 pieces, roll out each piece into a circle, and place on a lightly greased baking sheet. Meanwhile, heat 1 tablespoon olive oil in a large saucepan, add ⅓ cup dry white wine and 12 oz scrubbed clams, cover, and cook for 5 minutes, until the clams have opened. Discard any that do not open. Remove the meat from the shells. Stir 1 tablespoon lemon juice into 2 cups prepared fresh tomato sauce along with a pinch of dried red pepper flakes. Spread this over the prepared pizza crusts. Sprinkle with 8 oz mozzarella cut into strips and cook in a preheated oven, at 425°F, for 12 minutes, until golden and crisp. Sprinkle the cooked clams over the pizzas and bake for another 30 seconds to heat through.

20 Seared Monkfish with Spiced Beans

Serves 4

3 tablespoons olive oil
4 oz chorizo, chopped
1 onion, chopped
2 garlic cloves, finely chopped
½ cup dry white wine
⅓ cup light cream
2 (15 oz) cans cannellini beans, rinsed and drained
3 cups fresh white bread crumbs
pinch of dried red pepper flakes
1 thyme sprig, chopped
1 lb monkfish tail, cut into medallions
¼ cup lemon juice
salt and black pepper

- Heat 1 tablespoon olive oil in a saucepan, add the chorizo, and cook for 3–5 minutes, until golden. Remove the chorizo from the pan. Add the onion and cook for 5 minutes, until softened, then add the garlic and cook for another 1 minute. Pour in the wine and let simmer until reduced by half.

- Add the cream and the beans, return the chorizo to the pan, and season with salt and black pepper. Cook for another 5 minutes, adding a little water, if needed, and spoon into an ovenproof dish. Mix together the bread crumbs, red pepper flakes, and thyme and sprinkle with the beans. Drizzle with 1 tablespoon olive oil and cook under a hot broiler for 3–5 minutes, until golden and bubbling.

- Meanwhile, heat the remaining oil in a large, nonstick skillet. Season the monkfish and cook for 2–3 minutes on each side, until opaque and just cooked through. Remove from the skillet, add the lemon juice, and swirl around the skillet. Arrange the fish on plates with a spoonful of the beans and pour some of the juices in the skillet over them to serve.

10 Monkfish and Chorizo with Beans

Season 1 lb monkfish medallions and drizzle with olive oil. Cook under a preheated hot broiler for 3 minutes. Turn over and top each with a thin slice of chorizo. Cook for another 1–2 minutes, until the fish is cooked through. Mix 2 (15 oz) cans cannellini beans, rinsed and drained, with ⅓ cup olive oil, the juice and grated rind of 1 lemon, and 1 tablespoon chopped onion. Add 3 cups arugula and serve with the fish.

30 Monkfish Wrapped in Chorizo

Tear off a large sheet of plastic wrap and cover with about 20 thin slices of chorizo, overlapping the slices slightly. Cut 1 lb monkfish lengthwise into 2 fillets. Lay a fillet on top of the chorizo, then place the other fillet on top the other way around, top to tail. Use the plastic wrap to lift the chorizo up and over the monkfish to cover it tightly. Remove the plastic wrap and place the fish in a shallow roasting pan. Cook in a preheated oven, at 400°F, for 20–25 minutes, until the chorizo is crisp and the fish is cooked through. Simmer 2 (15 oz) cans rinsed and drained cannellini beans in ⅓ cup each heavy cream and chicken stock for 5 minutes, season to taste, then use an immersion blender to blend together and form mashed beans. Cut the fish into thick slices and serve with the beans.

Tomato and Feta Pilaf with Shrimp

Serves 4

3 tablespoons olive oil
1 onion, finely chopped
2 garlic cloves, crushed
1½ cups long grain rice
½ cup dry white wine
1 (14½ oz) can diced tomatoes
2 cups fish or chicken stock
1 lb large, raw shrimp with shells
¼ cup ouzo (optional)
handful of chopped oregano
½ cup crumbled feta cheese
pinch of dried red pepper flakes
salt and black pepper

- Heat 2 tablespoons olive oil in a large saucepan, add the onion, and cook for 5 minutes, until softened. Stir in the garlic and cook for another 30 seconds. Add the rice and stir around the pan until well coated. Pour in the wine and let simmer for 2–3 minutes, until reduced by half.

- Add the tomatoes and stock, season, and bring to a boil. Let cook for 10 minutes, until most of the liquid has boiled away, then turn down the heat to low, cover, and cook for 5 minutes, until the rice is soft.

- Meanwhile, heat the remaining oil in a large skillet. Add the shrimp and cook for 2 minutes, until turning golden. Turn over and carefully pour over the ouzo, if using. Cook for another 2–3 minutes, until the shrimp are cooked through and the ouzo has reduced. Season to taste. Transfer the rice to plates, arrange the shrimp on top, and then sprinkle with the oregano, feta, and red pepper flakes to serve.

---

10 **Spicy Shrimp and Tomato Pasta with Feta** Add 1 lb fresh penne pasta to a large saucepan of lightly salted boiling water and cook according to the package directions. Add 12 oz large, raw peeled shrimp for the last 3 minutes of cooking. Drain, reserving a little cooking water, and return to the pan. Stir in 8 halved cherry tomatoes, a pinch of dried red pepper flakes, 3 tablespoons olive oil, ⅔ cup crumbled feta cheese, and a little cooking water, if needed. Sprinkle with a handful of parsley leaves.

20 **Shrimp, Tomato, and Feta Stew** Heat 1 tablespoon olive oil in a saucepan, add 1 finely chopped onion, and cook for 5 minutes, until softened. Stir in 1 crushed garlic clove and cook for 30 seconds, then add 1 cup chopped tomatoes and cook for 5 minutes, until the tomatoes have softened. Pour in ⅔ cup chicken or fish stock and simmer for another 5 minutes. Then add 12 oz large, raw peeled shrimp and cook for 3–5 minutes, until just cooked through. Season to taste and sprinkle with chopped dill and parsley along with ½ cup crumbled feta cheese before serving with crusty bread.

 # Tandoori Salmon with Yogurt Sauce

Serves 4

2 tablespoons tandoori paste
⅔ cup plain yogurt
1 teaspoon grated fresh
 ginger root
4 salmon steaks
½ cucumber, finely chopped
finely grated rind and juice of
 ½ lime
handful of fresh mint, chopped
½ teaspoon cumin seeds
1 tablespoon vegetable oil
1 carrot, cut into matchsticks
½ red onion, sliced
¼ green cabbage, shredded
handful of fresh cilantro, chopped
salt and black pepper

- Mix together the tandoori paste with 2 tablespoons yogurt and ½ teaspoon ginger and smear all over the salmon steaks. Set aside to marinate for 5–10 minutes.

- Meanwhile, mix together the remaining yogurt with the cucumber, lime rind, and mint and season. Put the cumin seeds in a dry saucepan and cook for 30 seconds, until aromatic. Whisk together the remaining ginger with the lime juice, oil, and toasted cumin seeds to make a salad dressing. In a separate bowl, toss the carrot, onion, cabbage, and cilantro with the dressing.

- Cook the salmon under a preheated hot broiler for 3–5 minutes, until lightly charred. Turn over and cook for another 3 minutes, until browned and cooked through. Serve with the salad and the yogurt sauce.

 ### Salmon Salad with Yogurt Dressing

Thinly slice ½ cucumber and toss together with 5 cups mixed salad greens and 8 oz flaked, poached salmon. In a small bowl, stir together ⅓ cup plain yogurt with 1 tablespoon oil, 1 finely chopped red chile, 1 crushed garlic clove, and 1 teaspoon grated ginger. Add 1 tablespoon lime juice, season, and drizzle the dressing over the salad. Serve with crusty bread.

Salmon Kedgeree with Yogurt

Heat 1 tablespoon vegetable oil in a large saucepan and cook 1 finely chopped onion for 5 minutes, until softened. Add 2 crushed garlic cloves, 1 teaspoon grated fresh ginger root, and 1 teaspoon each ground coriander and cumin, a pinch of turmeric, and 4 cardamom pods. Cook for 30 seconds, then add 1½ cups long grain rice. Stir around the pan until well coated. Pour in 2½ cups fish or chicken stock, season to taste, bring to a boil, and simmer for 10 minutes, until most of the liquid has boiled away. Cover and cook for 5 minutes. Meanwhile, heat a saucepan of water until boiling. Add 8 quails' eggs, and cook for 4 minutes, drain, cool under cold running water, and remove the shells. Halve the eggs and stir into the rice with 8 oz chopped smoked salmon and 2 tablespoons diced butter. Spoon onto serving plates, drizzle with ¼ cup plain yogurt, and sprinkle with dried red pepper flakes and chopped fresh cilantro.

FOO-FISH-FEX

Italian Fish Stew

Serves 4

3 tablespoons olive oil
1 leek, sliced
4 garlic cloves, sliced
1 teaspoon fennel seeds
2 tablespoons tomato paste
½ cup dry white wine
1¼ cups fish stock
handful of oregano, chopped
2 cups halved cherry tomatoes
10 oz sea bream fillet
1 lb mussels
8 large, cooked shrimp with shells
5 oz squid, cut into rings

To serve

chopped parsley
crusty bread

- Heat the oil in a large saucepan, add the leek, and cook for 3–5 minutes, until soft. Stir in the garlic and fennel seeds and cook for 30 seconds. Stir in the tomato paste and cook for another 1 minute. Add the wine and let simmer for 1–2 minutes, then pour in the stock and let simmer for 5 minutes.

- Add the oregano, tomatoes, sea bream, and mussels. Cover and cook for 3 minutes. Add the shrimp and cook for another 2 minutes. Discard any mussels that do not open. Stir in the squid and heat through. Sprinkle with the parsley before serving with plenty of crusty bread.

---

10 Grilled Fish with Fennel and Tomato Salsa Finely chop 1 fennel bulb and mix together with ¼ cup extra virgin olive oil, a handful of chopped basil, and 6 chopped sun-dried tomatoes. Season to taste. Rub 1 tablespoon oil over 4 thin fish fillets. Cook on a hot ridged grill pan for 2–3 minutes on each side, until just cooked through. Spoon the salsa over the fish and serve.

30 Whole Sea Bream Baked in Tomato and Fennel Sauce Heat a large skillet, add 3 tablespoons olive oil and 2 chopped fennel bulbs, and cook for 5 minutes, until softened. Add 3 sliced garlic cloves and 1 chopped red chile and cook for 30 seconds. Pour in ½ cup dry white wine and let simmer for 2 minutes. Pour in 1¼ cups fish stock and bring to a simmer. Stir in 16 cherry tomatoes and a handful of oregano leaves and season to taste. Place 2 scaled and gutted sea bream in a deep roasting pan, pour the sauce over the fish, cover, and cook in a preheated oven, at 400°F, for 20 minutes or until the fish is cooked through. Sprinkle with some more oregano leaves before serving.

30 Crab and Corn Cakes with Red Pepper Mayonnaise

Serves 4

2 red bell peppers
3 tablespoons olive oil
1⅓ cups frozen corn kernels, defrosted
2 scallions, chopped
1 egg, lightly beaten
¼ cup mayonnaise
1 lb freshly picked crabmeat
½ cup dried bread crumbs
⅓ cup cornmeal
chipotle sauce, to taste
salt and black pepper

· Rub the bell peppers with 1 tablespoon oil and cook under a preheated hot broiler for 15 minutes, turning often, until charred all over. Put in a plastic bag and let cool a little, then peel away the skin and discard the seeds and cores.

· Mix together the corn, scallions, egg, and 2 tablespoons mayonnaise. Carefully stir in the crabmeat and season to taste. Form the mixture into small cakes, using your hands. Sprinkle the bread crumbs and cornmeal over a plate, and dip each cake into the crumbs until well coated. Transfer to a plate and let firm in the freezer for 5 minutes.

· Blend together the roasted bell peppers and remaining mayonnaise in a food processor until smooth and add chipotle sauce to taste. Heat the remaining oil in a large, nonstick skillet and cook the cakes for 2–3 minutes on each side, until crisp and golden. Serve with the red pepper mayonnaise.

---

1 Crab and Red Pepper Tostadas

Brush 4 corn tortillas with oil and cook them on a hot ridged grill pan for 30 seconds on each side, until lightly charred and crisp. Chop 4 tomatoes and mix together with 1 chopped roasted red pepper, the juice of ½ lime, and a large handful of chopped fresh cilantro. Season to taste. Place the tortillas on plates. Sprinkle with ¼ shredded iceberg lettuce. Divide 12 oz freshly picked crabmeat among them, top with sliced avocado, and spoon the red pepper and tomato salsa over the top to serve.

2 Spicy Crab and Corn Soup

Remove the kernels from 3 corn cobs using a sharp knife. Put the kernels and cobs in a large saucepan with 5 cups chicken stock and simmer for 10 minutes. Discard the cobs and remove a large spoonful of the kernels. Puree the mixture with an immersion blender or food processor until smooth, then stir in 1 tablespoon soy sauce, 1 teaspoon grated fresh ginger root, and 1 chopped chile. Simmer the soup for 5 minutes. Return the corn kernels to the pan together with 8 oz freshly picked crabmeat, 2 chopped scallions, and a handful of chopped fresh cilantro. Serve immediately.

Hot-Smoked Salmon and Watercress Pasta

Serves 4

1 lb fresh linguine

⅓ cup dry white wine

½ cup crème fraîche
   or heavy cream

3 hot-smoked salmon fillets,
   flaked

finely grated rind of ½ lemon

1 bunch watercress
   or 2 cups arugula

salt and black pepper

- Heat a large saucepan of lightly salted water until boiling. Cook the linguine according to the package directions, then drain and return to the pan, reserving a little of the cooking water.

- Bring the white wine to a boil in a saucepan, stir through the crème fraîche, and cook for 1–2 minutes, until reduced by half. Add the salmon to the pasta along with the crème fraîche sauce and lemon rind. Stir together, adding a little cooking water to loosen, if needed, and season to taste. Just before serving, toss through the watercress.

---

2 Baked Salmon with Watercress Sauce

Rub olive oil over 4 salmon fillets, season, and place on a baking sheet. Cook in a preheated oven, at 375°F, for 12–15 minutes, until just cooked through. Meanwhile, heat 1 tablespoon oil in a saucepan, add 1 chopped shallot, and cook for 3 minutes, until softened. Pour in ⅓ cup dry white wine and let simmer until nearly boiled away. Stir in ½ cup crème fraîche or heavy cream, and season. Blend in a blender with 3 bunches (5 oz) watercress or 1 (5 oz) package arugula until smooth. Let cool. Lightly whip ½ cup heavy cream, then stir it in the watercress mixture and spoon the sauce over the fish.

3 Salmon and Watercress Cakes

Peel and chop 2 potatoes, boil in a saucepan of salted water for 10–12 minutes, until soft, then coarsely mash and let cool a little. Mix the potato with 1 lb flaked poached salmon, 1 egg yolk, and 1½ bunches finely chopped watercress leaves or 3 cups finely chopped arugula. Season to taste and use your hands to shape the mixture into 8 fish cakes. Set aside in the refrigerator for 5–10 minutes, until firm. Dust each cake with a little flour. Put 1 beaten egg in a shallow dish and 3 cups fresh bread crumbs in another. Dip the cakes in the egg and then the bread crumbs, coating all over.

Heat 2 tablespoons oil in a large, nonstick skillet, add the fish cakes, and cook for 3–5 minutes, until golden. Turn over and cook for another 3–5 minutes, until golden and cooked through. Serve with lemon wedges.

20 Roasted Hake with Tomatoes and Pistou

Serves 4

4 thick hake steaks
¼ cup pitted ripe black olives
½ cup olive oil
8 cherry tomatoes
2 garlic cloves, peeled
bunch of basil, stems discarded
salt and black pepper
new potatoes, to serve

- Place the hake in a large roasting pan and sprinkle with the olives. Drizzle with 1 tablespoon oil, season, and bake in a preheated oven, at 400°F, for 12–15 minutes, until the fish is just cooked through. For the last 5 minutes of the cooking time, add the tomatoes to the roasting pan and drizzle with another tablespoon of oil.

- Meanwhile, put the garlic in a small food processor with a little salt and the basil and blend until a paste forms. Add the remaining oil, a little at a time, and blend to incorporate.

- Arrange the fish on plates with some boiled potatoes, and drizzle with the sauce to serve.

---

10 Grilled Hake with Olive Basil Salsa

Rub 1 tablespoon olive oil over 4 hake steaks, season, and cook on a smoking ridged grill pan for 5 minutes on each side, until just cooked through. Meanwhile, mix together 1 crushed garlic clove, 1 chopped tomato, ¼ cup chopped, pitted olives, ½ teaspoon red wine vinegar, a handful of chopped basil, and ¼ cup olive oil. Season and spoon the salsa over the fish to serve.

30 Summery Hake and Tomato Stew

Heat 2 tablespoons olive oil in a large, deep skillet, add 1 sliced onion and 1 sliced fennel bulb, and cook for 7 minutes, until softened. Stir in 1 teaspoon tomato paste and 1 crushed garlic clove, then add ½ cup dry white wine. Let boil until reduced by half. Add 1 (14½ oz) can diced tomatoes and a strip of orange rind. Let simmer for 5–10 minutes, then add 4 hake steaks, season, cover, and cook for 12–15 minutes or until the fish is just cooked through. Sprinkle with some chopped basil and serve.

30 Smoked Haddock and Spinach Tart

Serves 4

375 g (12 oz) skinless, boneless smoked haddock
150 g (5 oz) frozen leaf spinach
125 ml (4 fl oz) crème fraîche
3 eggs, beaten
2 scallions, sliced
375 g (12 oz) ready-rolled puff pastry
salt and black pepper

- Put the haddock in a pan, cover with boiling water and simmer for 3 minutes. Remove the fish from the pan and flake. Pour boiling water over the spinach until wilted, then squeeze away all the excess water.

- Mix together the crème fraîche, beaten eggs (reserving 1 tablespoon) and scallions and season well. Mix half this mixture with the spinach. Unwrap the pastry onto a baking sheet. Score a 1 cm (½ inch) border around the edges with a sharp knife and brush the border with the reserved egg.

- Spoon the spinach mixture into the center of the tart and sprinkle the haddock on top. Spoon over the remaining crème fraîche mixture and bake in a preheated oven, at 200°C (400°F), Gas Mark 6, for 20 minutes or until golden and cooked through.

---

10 Smoked Haddock and Spinach Gnocchi

Place 300 g (10 oz) skinless, boneless smoked haddock in a pan, cover with boiling water and simmer for 5 minutes, until just cooked through, then break the fish into large flakes. Heat a large pan of lightly salted boiling water and cook 500 g (1 lb) gnocchi according to the package directions. Add 150 g (5 oz) baby spinach leaves, drain and return to the pan. Add the haddock along with 75 ml (3 fl oz) crème fraîche and 1 teaspoon wholegrain mustard. Stir to coat and serve.

20 Smoked Haddock and Spinach Gratin

Put 4 small boneless smoked haddock fillets on a lightly greased baking sheet. Heat 1 tablespoon each butter and oil in a large skillet, add 200 g (7 oz) baby spinach and cook for 2–3 minutes, until starting to wilt. Drain and mix with 125 ml (4 fl oz) crème fraîche and a couple of tablespoons of milk until smooth. Spoon over the haddock and bake in a preheated oven, at 200°C (400°F), Gas Mark 6, for 12–15 minutes, until the fish is just cooked through.

20 Spicy Shrimp and Coconut Curry

Serves 4

1 teaspoon cumin seeds
3 cardamom pods
2 onions, coarsely chopped
¼ cup vegetable oil
1 bay leaf
6 curry leaves
1 inch piece of fresh ginger root,
  peeled and chopped
3 garlic cloves, peeled
½ teaspoon ground turmeric
1 red chile, seeded and chopped
1 cup coconut milk
8 cherry tomatoes, halved
1 lb raw shrimp, peeled
1 tablespoon butter
fresh cilantro leaves, chopped
boiled rice, to serve

- Put the cumin and cardamom in a small skillet and cook for 30 seconds, until aromatic. Remove and set aside. Blend the onions and 2 tablespoons oil in a food processor until smooth. Heat the remaining oil in a saucepan, add the onion paste, bay leaf, and curry leaves, and cook for 7–10 minutes, until light brown.

- Meanwhile, blend the ginger and garlic in a small food processor until smooth. Add to the pan with the toasted spices, turmeric, chile, coconut milk, tomatoes, and ⅔ cup water. Simmer for 5 minutes, then add the shrimp and cook for 3 minutes, until cooked through. Stir in the butter until melted. Sprinkle with the cilantro leaves and serve with plain rice.

10 Seared Shrimp with Coconut Salad

Mix 5 teaspoons ground cumin and a pinch of ground turmeric with 1 tablespoon oil. Rub over 1 lb raw, peeled shrimp. Season, then cook on a smoking ridged grill pan for 1–2 minutes on each side, until pink and cooked through. Whisk 3 tablespoons oil with 2 tablespoons lime juice and a pinch of sugar and season. Toss through 5 cups salad greens, ½ sliced cucumber, and 1 chopped red chile. Sprinkle with ⅓ cup lightly toasted dry shredded coconut and serve with the shrimp.

30 Spicy Baked Shrimp Cakes

Put 1 shallot in a food processor with 2 tablespoons oil and blend to a smooth paste. Heat 1 tablespoon vegetable oil in a saucepan and cook the onion paste for 7 minutes, until golden brown. Meanwhile, blend ½ inch fresh ginger root and 2 peeled garlic cloves until smooth and stir into the pan for the last 2 minutes of cooking. Let cool a little. Blend 1 lb raw, peeled shrimp and 1 tablespoon dry shredded coconut together with the cooled onion paste, 1 teaspoon ground cumin, a pinch of ground turmeric, and a handful of fresh cilantro to make a chunky batter. Season well. Lightly grease a 12-cup muffin pan and divide the batter among the cups. Cook in a preheated oven, at 350°F, for 12–15 minutes, until golden and cooked through.

# 3️⃣ Charred Tuna with Peperonata

Serves 4

⅓ cup olive oil
1 onion, thinly sliced
3 garlic cloves, chopped
3 red bell peppers, halved
½ teaspoon dried red
   pepper flakes
1 (14½ oz) can tomatoes
4 tuna steaks
salt and black pepper
arugula salad, to serve

- Heat ¼ cup oil in a skillet, add the onion, garlic, and bell peppers, and cook over low heat for 10 minutes, until soft and golden. Add the red pepper flakes and tomatoes, season to taste, cover, and let simmer for 10 minutes. Uncover and cook for another 5 minutes, until soft and most of the liquid has boiled away.

- Meanwhile, rub the remaining oil over the tuna steaks and season thoroughly. Heat a ridged grill pan until smoking and cook the tuna steaks for 2–3 minutes on each side, until charred but still pink inside. Serve the tuna with the peperonata and an arugula salad.

1️⃣ Tuna Pasta with Red Pepper Pesto

Cook 1 lb fresh spaghetti in a large saucepan of lightly boiling salted water according to the package directions. Drain, reserving 1 tablespoon of water, and return to the pan. Blend ½ cup toasted silvered almonds in a food processor with 2 roasted red bell peppers, 1 tablespoon olive oil, and ¼ cup crème fraîche or sour cream. Season to taste. Add the pesto to the pasta with the cooking water, if needed, and 1 (5 oz) can tuna, drained. Stir through 3 cups arugula leaves and serve.

2️⃣ Spicy Tuna Red Pepper Stew

Thoroughly drain 1 (12 oz) can of tuna and mix with 1 egg yolk, 1 chopped scallion, 1 chopped roasted red pepper, and a pinch of dried red pepper flakes. Season well. Use your hands to form the mixture into about 12 walnut-size balls. Heat 2 tablespoons vegetable oil in a large, nonstick skillet, add the tuna balls and 1 chopped red bell pepper, and cook for 5 minutes, turning often, until golden. Stir in 3 sliced garlic cloves and cook for 30 seconds. Pour in 1 (14½ oz) can tomatoes and let simmer for 10 minutes. Sprinkle with chopped basil leaves and serve with rice or crusty bread.

 Thai-Style Squid Salad

Serves 4

¼ cup firmly packed light
  brown sugar
¼ cup boiling water
1 garlic clove, crushed
2 teaspoons finely chopped
  fresh ginger root
1 red chile, chopped
finely grated rind and juice of 1 lime
3 tablespoons Thai fish sauce
12 oz prepared squid
1 tablespoon oil
½ red onion, thinly sliced
8 cherry tomatoes, halved
1 (7 oz) package salad greens
handful of fresh cilantro
salt and black pepper

- Stir together the sugar and water until the sugar dissolves. Put the garlic, ginger, chile, and lime rind into a bowl and pour in the sugar syrup. Put in the refrigerator to cool, then stir through the lime juice and fish sauce.

- Meanwhile, cut the squid pouches in half. Score a crisscross pattern across the inside of the squid with a sharp knife, being careful not to cut all the way through, then cut into bite-size pieces. Rub the oil over the squid and season well. Cook on a smoking ridged grill pan for 1–2 minutes, until charred and just cooked through.

- Put the onion, tomatoes, salad greens, and cilantro on a plate. Arrange the squid on top and drizzle with the dressing before serving.

---

2 Thai Seafood Broth with Noodles

Heat 1 tablespoon oil in a saucepan, add 2 tablespoons Thai red curry paste, and cook for 1 minute. Pour in 3 cups fish stock and bring to a boil. Add 1 lemon grass stalk, 2 lime leaves, 1 teaspoon granulated sugar, and 1 tablespoon Thai fish sauce. Let simmer for 10 minutes. Remove the lemon grass and lime leaves. Pour in 1¾ cups coconut milk and heat through. Add 8 oz raw peeled shrimp and 2 cups sugar snap peas and cook for 2 minutes. Then add 1 lb rice noodles, cooked, and heat for 1 minute. Stir in 5 oz sliced squid, cook for another 30 seconds, then ladle into bowls. Top with a handful of chopped fresh cilantro and a handful of bean sprouts.

3 Marinated Thai Squid

Slice 10 oz squid into rings. Put in a bowl with the juice of ½ orange and 1 lime, and 2 tablespoons Thai fish sauce. Let marinate for 25 minutes, until the squid turns opaque, then toss with 1 tablespoon finely chopped red onion, ½ sliced red chile, a handful of chopped fresh cilantro, and 8 halved cherry tomatoes. Mix a little of the marinating liquid with 2 tablespoons olive oil, season, and toss through 5 cups aromatic salad greens. Add the drained squid and serve.

30 Monkfish with Saffron Risotto and Gremolata

Serves 4

3 tablespoons olive oil
1 onion, finely chopped
2 garlic cloves, finely chopped
2 teaspoons tomato paste
1½ cups risotto rice
½ cup dry white wine
pinch of saffron threads
3¾ cups hot chicken or fish stock
1 lb skinless, boneless
   monkfish tail
finely grated rind of 1 lemon
handful of parsley, chopped
salt and black pepper

- Heat 2 tablespoons oil in a large saucepan, add the onion, and cook for 5 minutes, until softened. Stir in 1 chopped garlic clove and the tomato paste and cook for 30 seconds. Stir in the rice and cook for 2 minutes, until the rice is well coated.

- Pour the wine into the pan and cook until it has simmered away. Add the saffron, then gradually stir in the hot stock, a little at a time, stirring frequently and letting the rice absorb the stock before adding more.

- Meanwhile, heat the remaining oil in a large skillet. Cut the monkfish into large cubes, add to the skillet, season, and cook for 1–2 minutes on each side, until golden. Remove from the skillet. Add the remaining stock to the rice along with the fish and cook for another 5 minutes, until the rice and fish are cooked through.

- Mix together the remaining chopped garlic with the lemon rind and parsley. Spoon the rice and fish onto plates and sprinkle with the gremolata to serve.

---

10 Gremolata Grilled Monkfish with Saffron Mayonnaise Cut a 1 lb monkfish tail into thick slices. Mix 1 crushed garlic clove, the finely grated rind of 1 lemon, and a handful of parsley with 1 tablespoon olive oil. Season and smear the mixture all over the fish and cook on a smoking ridged grill pan for 3 minutes on each side. Meanwhile, pour 1 tablespoon boiling water over a pinch of saffron threads and let sit for 1 minute. Crush 1 garlic clove and mix with ⅓ cup mayonnaise. Add the saffron water and a good squeeze of lemon juice. Divide 1 (5 oz) package arugula leaves among 4 plates. Drizzle with the saffron mayonnaise, top with the grilled fish, and serve with plenty of crusty bread.

20 Baked Saffron Monkfish Fillets Pour 1 tablespoon boiling water over a pinch of saffron threads and let sit for 1 minute. Mix with ⅓ cup plain yogurt, 1 teaspoon ground cumin, a pinch of dried red pepper flakes, 1 crushed garlic clove, and 1 tablespoon lemon juice. Season and rub over 4 (7 oz) monkfish fillets. Marinate for 5–10 minutes. Shake off any excess marinade, drizzle with oil, and cook in a preheated oven, at 400°F, for 10 minutes, until cooked through.

20 Cod Fillets with Tomatoes and Salsa Verde

Serves 4

4 thick cod fillets
4 plum tomatoes, halved
1 tablespoon olive oil
salt and black pepper

Salsa verde

2 canned anchovy fillets
1 garlic clove, peeled
1 teaspoon capers, drained
1 tablespoon Dijon mustard
1 tablespoon white wine vinegar
½ cup extra virgin olive oil
large handful of parsley,
   finely chopped
large handful of basil,
   finely chopped

- Season the cod and put it in a lightly greased baking dish along with the tomatoes. Drizzle with the oil and cook in a preheated oven, at 400°F, for 15 minutes, until the fish is opaque and just cooked through.

- Chop the anchovies, garlic, and capers finely to form a coarse paste. Mix together with the mustard and vinegar, then stir in the oil, followed by the herbs.

- Drizzle the sauce over the fish fillets and tomatoes to serve.

---

10 Salsa Verde Cod Skewers

Cube 1 lb thick, skinless, boneless cod fillets and toss together with 3 tablespoons olive oil, the finely grated rind of 1 lemon, 1 crushed garlic clove, and large handful each of chopped parsley and basil. Season well and thread onto skewers. Cook on a hot ridged grill pan for 3 minutes on each side, until just cooked through. Squeeze a little lemon juice over the fish and serve.

30 Baked Cod and Tomatoes with

Herb Sauce Lightly oil 4 large pieces of aluminum foil. Thinly slice 1 onion and divide among the sheets. Place 4 thick cod fillets on top, then sprinkle with 4 sliced tomatoes, season, and add a thyme sprig and a little more oil to each. Carefully fold up each piece of foil, leaving a little gap, and place on a baking sheet. Pour 2 tablespoons dry white wine into each package and seal, leaving a little space around the fish. Bake in a preheated oven, at 400°F, for 20 minutes, until just cooked through. Meanwhile, place 1 finely chopped shallot, 1 tablespoon white wine vinegar, and 2 tablespoons dry white wine in a saucepan and boil until reduced to 2 tablespoons. Cut 1 stick cold butter into cubes and whisk into the sauce, a cube at a time, until the sauce is thick and creamy. Add a handful each of chopped parsley and basil and 1 teaspoon capers. Season and spoon the sauce over the fish to serve.

Salmon, Dill, and Rice Packages

Serves 4

2 cups cooked plain rice
2 scallions, chopped
finely grated rind of 1 lemon
handful of dill, chopped
4 thin skinless, boneless lightly
  smoked salmon fillets
4 tablespoons butter, melted
3 tablespoons olive oil
4 sheets of phyllo pastry
salt and black pepper
peas and sugar snap peas,
  to serve

- Mix together the rice, scallions, lemon rind, and dill. Cut the salmon into large chunks and stir through the rice.

- Stir together the melted butter and oil. Unwrap 1 pastry sheet, leaving the remainder covered with a damp, but not wet, sheet of paper towel. Brush all over with the butter mixture, then sprinkle one-quarter of the rice mixture along one short side. Fold in the long sides of the pastry and roll up to enclose the filling completely.

- Place on a baking sheet and brush with some more butter. Repeat with the remaining mixture and pastry. Bake in a preheated oven, at 425°F, for 15 minutes, until golden and crispy. Serve with peas and sugar snap peas.

Salmon and Rice Salad

Heat 1 (9 oz) package precooked rice according to the package directions, transfer to a strainer, and cool under cold running water. Cook 1 cup fava beans in a saucepan of boiling water for 3 minutes, until soft, drain, and cool under cold running water. Stir with the rice and 5 oz flaked hot-smoked salmon. Add 1 chopped scallion, a handful of chopped dill, the finely grated rind of ½ lemon, and 1 tablespoon lemon juice.

Salmon Pasta Casserole with Crunchy Lemon Dill Topping

Cook 1 lb penne according to the package directions, drain, and return to the saucepan. Stir through 1 cup crème fraîche or heavy cream and ⅓ cup water to make a smooth sauce. Add 5 oz smoked salmon cut into strips and transfer to a baking dish. Mix together ¾ cup dry bread crumbs, the finely grated rind of 1 lemon, and a handful of chopped dill. Sprinkle the mixture over the pasta and drizzle with 1 tablespoon melted butter. Cook in a preheated oven, at 400°F, for 15 minutes, until bubbling and golden.

Baked Sea Bass with Tomatoes, Olives, and Oregano

Serves 4

3 lb whole sea bass,
  scaled and gutted
2 tablespoons olive oil
2 oregano sprigs, chopped
pinch of dried red pepper flakes
1 lemon, sliced
8 cherry tomatoes
¾ cup pitted Kalamata olives
salt and black pepper

To serve

olive-oil roasted potatoes
green salad

- Use a sharp knife to cut 3 slashes across each side of the fish. Mix together the olive oil, oregano, and red pepper flackes, and rub all over the fish. Season well, place in an ovenproof dish, sprinkle around the lemon slices, and bake in a preheated oven, at 425°F, for 10 minutes.

- Add the tomatoes and olives and return to the oven for 10–15 minutes, until the fish is just cooked through. Serve with new potatoes roasted in olive oil and a green salad.

---

1 **Grilled Sea Bass with Tomato and Olive Sauce** Brush 1 tablespoon olive oil over 4 sea bass fillets and season well. Cook, skin side down, on a smoking ridged grill pan for 5 minutes, until crisp. Turn over and cook for another 3 minutes or until the fish is just cooked through. Meanwhile, toss together 1 chopped tomato, 2 teaspoons red wine vinegar, 3 tablespoons olive oil, ½ cup coarsely chopped pitted olives, 1 teaspoon drained capers, and a handful of chopped oregano leaves. Season and drizzle the sauce over the fish to serve.

2 **Mediterranean Sea Bass Stew** Heat 2 tablespoons olive oil in a large casserole, add 1 finely chopped onion, and cook for 5 minutes, until softened. Add 1 chopped red bell pepper and cook for another 2 minutes. Stir in 2 crushed garlic cloves and 1 teaspoon tomato paste and cook for 30 seconds. Pour in ½ cup dry white wine and let simmer until reduced by half. Add 1 (14½ oz) can tomatoes and a pinch of sugar and let simmer for 2–3 minutes. Add 1 lb sea bass fillet, cut into chunks, and ½ cup pitted olives, season, and let cook for 2 minutes or until the fish is just cooked through. Stir through a handful of oregano leaves and serve.

Tea-Smoked Salmon

Serves 4

½ cup rice
½ cup firmly packed light
   brown sugar
⅓ cup tea leaves
4 salmon fillets
3 tablespoons rice wine vinegar
1 teaspoon granulated sugar
½ cucumber, sliced into thin
   ribbons
1 cup halved radishes
handful of bean sprouts
handful of fresh cilantro leaves,
   chopped
1 red chile, chopped

- Line a large wok with 4 sheets of aluminum foil. Put the rice, brown sugar, and tea leaves in the bottom of the wok. Turn on the extractor fan, place a tight-fitting lid on the wok, and heat over medium heat for about 5 minutes, until the mixture is smoking.

- Lightly season the salmon fillets. Put an oiled rack or steamer basket in the wok with the salmon fillets inside. Put the lid back on the wok and let smoke for 8–10 minutes, until the fish is just cooked through.

- Stir together the vinegar and granulated sugar until the sugar has dissolved. Toss together with the remaining ingredients and serve alongside the salmon fillets.

1 ○ Salmon Fillets Poached in Tea

Pour 4 cups boiling water over 4 green tea bags. Stir in a ¾ inch piece of fresh ginger root, peeled, and press down on the tea bags to extract the flavor. Put 4 salmon fillets in a shallow saucepan, pour the tea mixture over the fish, and simmer for 8 minutes, until the salmon is just cooked through. Remove from the poaching liquid and serve with a cucumber salad and plain rice.

3 ○ Tea-Smoked Salmon Fish Cakes

Peel and chop 2 potatoes, boil in a saucepan of salted water for 10–12 minutes, until soft, then coarsely mash and let cool a little. Prepare the tea-smoked salmon as above, then remove the skin and tear the fish into flakes. Mix together with the potatoes, 1 egg yolk, and a large handful of chopped fresh cilantro leaves. Form the mixture into 8 small fish cakes, dust all over with ⅔ cup all-purpose flour, and dip each cake in 1 beaten egg. Finally, coat in 1½ cups panko bread crumbs. Heat 2 tablespoons vegetable oil in a saucepan and cook the fish cakes for 3 minutes on each side, until golden. Serve with wedges of lime for squeezing over.

Prosciutto-Wrapped Scallops with Red Peppers and Beans

Serves 4

2–3 tablespoons olive oil
2 garlic cloves, finely chopped
2 (15 oz) cans cannellini beans,
 rinsed and drained
½ cup hot chicken stock
¼ cup light cream
lemon juice, to taste
1 red bell pepper, cut into wedges
12 slices of prosciutto
12 large prepared scallops
salt and black pepper
handful of arugula leaves,
 to serve

- Heat 1 tablespoon oil in a saucepan, add the garlic, and cook for 30 seconds. Add the beans, stock, and cream and cook for 3 minutes, until the beans are warmed through. Use an immersion blender to blend to a creamy paste, season, and add lemon juice to taste.

- Meanwhile, rub a little oil over the bell pepper and place on a smoking ridged grill pan. Cook for 2 minutes on each side, until charred and soft. Wrap a prosciutto slice around each scallop, securing with a toothpick, if needed. Rub over a little oil and cook on the grill pan with the bell pepper for 2 minutes on each side, until just cooked through. Serve with the beans and a few arugula leaves alongside.

2 Scallops with Salsa and Prosciutto

Rub 1 tablespoon olive oil over 2 red bell peppers and cook under a hot broiler for 12 minutes, turning occasionally, until charred. Place in a plastic bag and let cool a little, then remove the skin and seeds. Chop the flesh and mix with 1 tablespoon sherry vinegar, 3 tablespoons olive oil, and 1 teaspoon chopped thyme. Cook 4 slices of prosciutto in 1 tablespoon olive oil for 1 minute on each side, until crispy, then remove from the skillet. Add 12 large scallops to the pan and cook for 2 minutes on each side, until just cooked through. Chop the prosciutto, sprinkle with the scallops, and serve with the salsa.

3 Red Pepper and Scallop Paella

Heat 2 tablespoons olive oil in a large, deep saucepan, add 4 oz chopped chorizo, and cook for 2 minutes, until golden. Add 1 chopped onion and cook for 5 minutes, until softened. Stir in 2 chopped garlic cloves and cook for another 30 seconds. Add 1 chopped red bell pepper and 1½ cups paella or risotto rice and stir around the pan. Pour in 2½ cups chicken or fish stock and a pinch saffron threads. Stir to combine, season, then let simmer for 10 minutes, until most of the liquid has been absorbed. Add 8 oz clams to the pan along with 8 large, raw peeled shrimp. Cook for 5 minutes, until the seafood and rice are cooked through. Discard any clams that do not open. Add 12 baby scallops and stir through. Cook for another 1 minute, until the scallops are cooked, sprinkle with chopped parsley, and serve.

Sesame-Crusted Tuna with Ginger Dressing

Serves 6

1¾ lb 1piece of tuna
2 tablespoons vegetable oil
3 tablespoons white sesame seeds
3 tablespoons black sesame seeds
½ cucumber, sliced into ribbons
2 avocados, sliced
2 scallions, shredded
salt and black pepper

Dressing

1 garlic clove, crushed
1 chile, seeded and finely chopped
1 teaspoon finely chopped
   fresh ginger root
1 tablespoon soy sauce
juice of ½ lime
1 teaspoon grated orange rind
1 tablespoon honey
1 tablespoon sesame oil

- Season the tuna. Heat the oil in a large skillet, add the tuna, and cook for 3–5 minutes or until browned all over. Put the sesame seeds on a plate and press the seared tuna into them until well coated. Cook in a preheated oven, at 425°F, for 10–12 minutes, until browned, but still pink inside.

- Mix together the ingredients for the dressing. Cut the tuna into thick slices and arrange on serving plates with the cucumber slices, avocados, and scallions. Drizzle the dressing over the tuna to serve.

---

1 Tuna Carpaccio with Ginger Salad

Cut 1¼ lb fresh tuna into ½ inch steaks, put between 2 pieces of plastic wrap, and pound gently until thin. Arrange on serving plates. Whisk the juice of 1 orange and 1 lime and 1 teaspoon each finely chopped fresh ginger root, rice wine vinegar, and soy sauce. Toss through 1 (7 oz) package arugula leaves and 1¼ cups sliced radishes. Arrange on top of the tuna and sprinkle with toasted sesame seeds.

3 Slow-Cooked Tuna Steaks with Sesame Ginger Noodles

Rub 1 tablespoon olive oil over 6 large tuna steaks, place on a baking sheet, and cook in a preheated oven, at 225°F, for 20 minutes for rare. Meanwhile, cook 1¼ lb udon noodles according to the package directions. Drain and cool under cold running water. Heat 3 tablespoons oil in a wok, add 4 finely chopped garlic cloves, 3 sliced scallions, and 1 tablespoon finely chopped fresh ginger root, and cook for 30 seconds. Add the noodles to the pan with 1 cup cooked edamame beans and stir together with ¼ cup light soy sauce, 1 teaspoon sesame oil, and 1 tablespoon sesame seeds. Heat through and serve alongside the tuna steaks.

 Citrus-Roasted Salmon

Serves 4

1 tablespoon olive oil
1 onion, sliced into rings
2 oranges, sliced
2 lemons, sliced
handful of thyme sprigs
3 lb piece of salmon,
    divided into 2 fillets
½ cup dry white wine
4 tablespoons butter
salt and black pepper

To serve

crushed potatoes
green beans

- Brush a large baking sheet with the oil, place half the onion, orange, and lemon on top, and sprinkle with some thyme sprigs. Place a salmon fillet, skin side down, on top of the fruit, onion, and thyme. Put the remaining fruit, onion, and thyme on the fish and season well, then place the remaining salmon fillet on top. Tie some kitchen string around the fish to secure.

- Pour the wine over the fish and dot with the butter. Cook in a preheated oven, at 425°F, for 25 minutes or until just cooked through. Remove the fish to a serving plate.

- Transfer the juices and bottom layer of fruit to a strainer set over a bowl. Press any extra juice from the fruit and serve over the salmon with some crushed potatoes and beans.

1 Smoked Salmon with Chile Citrus

Dressing Arrange 10 oz smoked salmon on plates. Cut 2 ripe avocados into cubes and sprinkle them over the salmon with ¾ cup sliced radishes. In a small bowl, mix together the juice and finely grated rind of ½ lime with 3 tablespoons orange juice, 1 tablespoon soy sauce, 1 tablespoon granulated sugar, and 1 finely chopped red chile. Spoon the dressing over the salmon to serve.

2 Crispy Citrus Salmon

Toss the finely grated rind of 1 lemon and ⅓ orange with 1 cup dry bread crumbs. Stir in a handful of chopped basil. Rub 2 tablespoons olive oil over 4 large salmon fillets until well coated, season to taste, then press the bread crumbs all over the top of the fish and drizzle with a little more oil. Place on a baking sheet and cook in a preheated oven, at 400°F, for 12–15 minutes or until the fish is just cooked through.

20 Broiled Lobster with Herb Butter

Serves 4

1 stick butter, softened
1 garlic clove, crushed
1 tablespoon lemon juice
large handful of chopped parsley
large handful of chopped chives
2 cooked lobsters
salt and black pepper

To serve

green salad with fennel
potato wedges

- Mix together the butter, garlic, lemon juice, and herbs and season. Place in a sheet of plastic wrap, roll into a cylinder, and twist the ends to seal. Put in the freezer for 5 minutes to harden a little.

- Snap the claws away from the lobsters and crack the shell with the back of a heavy knife to remove the meat inside. Cut each lobster body in half lengthwise. Wash out the head cavities with cold water and divide the claw meat between them.

- Put the lobsters on a broiler pan, cut side up, slice the butter, and place on top. Cook under a preheated hot broiler for 5–7 minutes, until bubbling. Serve with green salad and potato wedges.

10 Lobster, Herb, and Chile Salad

Carefully remove the meat from 2 cooked lobster tails and thickly slice. Cut 2 avocados into thick slices and arrange on a plate with a handful of mixed salad greens and ½ cucumber cut into ribbons with a vegetable peeler. Place the lobster meat on top of the salad greens and vegetables. Whisk 2 tablespoons lemon juice with ¼ cup olive oil, a handful of chopped basil, and ½ finely chopped red chile. Season and drizzle it over the salad to serve.

30 Lobster with Creamy Herb Sauce

Cut 2 cooked lobsters in half lengthwise and remove the meat from the tails. Crack the claws, remove the meat, and cut into chunks. Melt 2 tablespoons butter in a saucepan, add 3 tablespoons all-purpose flour, and cook for 2 minutes. Whisk in 1¼ cups milk and let simmer for 5–7 minutes, until thickened. Heat 2 tablespoons butter in another saucepan, add 1 chopped shallot, and cook for 3 minutes, until soft. Add 1 crushed garlic clove, pour in ½ cup dry white wine, and cook for 5 minutes or until reduced down. Stir this into the white sauce, add ¼ cup heavy cream, season, and heat through. Take off the heat and add 2 egg yolks, the lobster meat, and a handful each of chopped tarragon and parsley. Put the lobster shells on a baking sheet and divide the lobster mixture between them. Sprinkle with some grated Parmesan cheese, then cook under a hot broiler for 5–7 minutes, until golden and bubbling.

QuickCook
Vegetarian

Recipes listed by cooking time

3

2

Baked Tomato and Spinach Puffs

Serves 4

¼ cup extra virgin olive oil,
  plus extra for greasing
6 sun-dried tomatoes
1 (5 oz) package baby leaf spinach
1⅔ cups ricotta cheese
3 eggs, beaten
¼ cup grated Parmesan cheese
½ cup chopped, pitted
  ripe black olives
1 tablespoon capers,
  rinsed and drained
handful of basil leaves, chopped
salt and black pepper

To serve

mixed salad
toasted pine nuts

- Lightly grease 4 dariole molds or ramekins. Place a tomato in the bottom of each and finely chop the remainder. Put the spinach in a strainer and pour boiling water over it until wilted, then squeeze out any excess liquid. Beat together the ricotta and eggs, preferably with an electric handheld mixer, for 1–2 minutes, until light and airy.

- Finely chop the spinach and stir into the ricotta along with the chopped tomatoes and Parmesan. Season to taste. Spoon the mixture into the prepared molds, place on a baking sheet, and bake in a preheated oven, at 375°F, for 20 minutes, until lightly puffed.

- Mix together the oil, olives, capers, and basil and season to taste. Ease the baked puffs out of the molds and place on serving plates. Drizzle with the sauce and serve with a mixed salad, sprinkled with toasted pine nuts.

1 Spinach and Tomato Pizza

Arrange 4 soft flour tortillas on nonstick baking sheets and spoon 1¼ cups fresh tomato sauce on top. Place 1 (5 oz) package baby spinach in a strainer and pour boiling water over it until wilted. Squeeze out excess liquid and then arrange on the sauce. Sprinkle with 4 oz sliced mozzarella cheese and ¼ cup ricotta cheese. Place under a preheated hot broiler and cook for 5 minutes, until the cheese has melted and the sauce is bubbling.

2 Roasted Tomato and Spinach Salad

Quarter 6 plum tomatoes and place on a baking sheet. Drizzle with 2 tablespoons olive oil, season, and cook in a preheated oven, at 400°F, for 15 minutes, until soft. Meanwhile, cook 1 cup green beans in lightly salted boiling water for 3–5 minutes, until just soft. Drain and cool under cold running water. Whisk together 1 tablespoon red wine vinegar, 3 tablespoons extra virgin olive oil, and 1 teaspoon Dijon mustard. Toss the dressing through 1 (5 oz) package baby spinach leaves and the beans. Arrange on a plate, top with the tomatoes, and sprinkle with ¼ cup ricotta cheese and some toasted pine nuts to serve.

20 Creamy Walnut and Arugula Pasta

Serves 4

1 lb orecchiette or other small
  pasta shapes
1 cup walnut pieces
1 garlic clove, crushed
¼ cup extra virgin olive oil
⅓ cup heavy cream
¼ cup grated Parmesan cheese
3½ cups arugula leaves
salt and black pepper

- Cook the orecchiette in a large saucepan of lightly salted boiling water according to the package directions.

- Meanwhile, place most of the walnuts, the garlic, oil, cream, and grated Parmesan in a small blender and blend until smooth. Season to taste.

- Drain the pasta, reserving a little of the cooking water, then stir through the walnut sauce, adding a little cooking water, if needed. Toss in the arugula leaves and transfer to serving bowls. Top with the reserved walnuts and serve immediately.

---

10 Pasta with Goat Cheese and Walnut

Sauce Mix 1 crushed garlic clove with 3 oz soft goat cheese, ⅓ cup cream cheese, ¼ cup chopped walnuts, and a large handful of chopped basil. Season to taste. Cook 1 lb fresh pasta in a large saucepan of lightly salted boiling water according to the package directions. Drain, reserving a little of the cooking water. Return to the pan and stir through the sauce, adding a little cooking water, if needed. Top with more basil and sprinkle with some more goat cheese to serve.

30 Gnocchi with Walnut, Chile, and Arugula Pesto

Cook 12 small, unpeeled potatoes (1¼ lb) in a large saucepan of boiling water for 15 minutes, until soft. Drain well, peel, and mash until smooth. Add 2⅓ cups all-purpose flour, a pinch of salt, and ½ cup grated Parmesan cheese and mix to a soft dough. Divide into 4 and roll into long cylinders. Cut into small pieces, about ¾ inch long, and press down gently on each one with the tines of a fork to make a ridged surface. Cook the gnocchi

in a large saucepan of lightly salted boiling water for about 3 minutes, until they rise to the surface of the pan. Remove with a slotted spoon. Meanwhile, blend ¾ cup toasted walnuts in a food processor with 3½ cups arugula leaves, 1 seeded and finely chopped chile, ½ cup grated Parmesan cheese, 1 crushed garlic clove, and ⅓ cup extra virgin olive oil. Season, toss the pesto through the gnocchi, and serve with some more arugula leaves sprinkled over the top.

FOO-VEGE-BOT

Zucchini and Feta Fritters

Serves 4

1 egg, lightly beaten
3 tablespoons all-purpose flour
2 tablespoons buttermilk
2 large zucchini, grated
handful of fresh dill, chopped
3 scallions, chopped
1 cup crumbled feta cheese
⅓ cup olive oil
toasted pita breads, to serve

Roasted pepper salad

2 roasted peppers, chopped
1 tablespoon lemon juice
2 tablespoons olive oil
handful of mint leaves, chopped

- Mix together the egg, flour, and buttermilk until smooth. Place the zucchini in a clean dish towel and squeeze to remove excess water, then mix into the batter along with the dill and scallions. Add the feta cheese.

- Heat half the oil in a large nonstick skillet. Add heaping tablespoons of the batter to the skillet and press down a little on each fritter with the back of the spoon to flatten slightly. Cook for 3 minutes, until golden brown, then turn and cook for another 2 minutes, until golden and cooked through. Drain on paper towels and keep warm. Repeat with the remaining batter and oil.

- Stir together the roasted peppers, lemon juice, oil and mint. Serve alongside the fritters with some toasted pita breads.

10 Tangy Couscous, Zucchini, and Feta

Salad Slice 2 zucchini into long, thin strips. Rub with 2 tablespoons olive oil and cook on a hot ridged grill pan for 1 minute on each side, until lightly charred. Place 1¾ cups couscous in a bowl and pour 1¾ cups hot vegetable stock over the grains. Cover and let sit for 5 minutes, then stir in ¼ cup lemon juice, ⅓ cup olive oil, and a handful each of chopped parsley and mint. Season and add 1⅓ cups sun-dried tomatoes and the zucchini. Sprinkle with ½ cup toasted pine nuts and ⅔ cup crumbled feta cheese.

30 Zucchini Frittata with Dill, Feta, and

Olive Salsa Heat 3 tablespoons olive oil in a large, nonstick skillet, add 1 finely chopped onion, and cook for 5 minutes, until softened. Meanwhile, shred 2 large zucchini. Place the zucchini in a clean dish towel and squeeze to remove excess water. Add to the skillet and cook for another 5 minutes, until soft and any water has evaporated. Turn the heat to low and pour in 6 eggs, beaten with a little salt. Cook for 10–15 minutes or until the eggs have set. Gently toss together a handful of dill with ½ cup crumbled feta cheese, ½ cup pitted olives, and 2 cups arugula, then add a squeeze of lemon juice and 1 tablespoon olive oil. Cut the frittata into wedges and serve with the salsa on top.

10 Spicy Tofu and Mushroom Stir-Fry

Serves 4

2 tablespoons vegetable oil
8 oz shiitake mushrooms,
 halved if large
1 leek (white only), thinly sliced
2 garlic cloves, chopped
2 teaspoons grated ginger root
3 tablespoons black bean sauce
1 teaspoon chili sauce
pinch of ground Sichuan pepper
1 tablespoon cornstarch
⅔ cup vegetable stock
2 tablespoons soy sauce
1 tablespoon rice wine vinegar
1 tablespoon granulated sugar
1⅓ cups cubed firm tofu
2 scallions, shredded
plain boiled rice, to serve

- Heat the oil in a large wok, add the mushrooms, and cook for 2 minutes. Add the leek and cook for another 2 minutes, until softened. Stir in the garlic and ginger, followed by the black bean and chili sauces and the Sichuan pepper.

- Mix together the cornstarch, stock, soy sauce, vinegar, and sugar and add to the wok. Carefully stir in the tofu. Let simmer for 2–3 minutes, until the sauce has thickened. Sprinkle with the scallions and serve with plain boiled rice.

20 Egg-Fried Tofu and Shiitake Rice

Boil 1¼ cups quick-cooking rice according to package directions, then drain. Heat 2 tablespoons oil in a wok, add ⅔ cup cubed firm tofu, and cook for 3 minutes. Remove from the wok. Add 5 oz shiitake mushrooms. Cook for 2 minutes, then add 2 chopped garlic cloves, 1 teaspoon grated fresh ginger root, and 2 chopped scallions. Cook for 1 minute. Crack 1 egg into the wok and stir until just cooked. Add the rice, tofu, ⅓ cup defrosted frozen peas, and 3 tablespoons soy sauce, stir, and serve.

30 Spicy Tofu Pockets

Cut 1¼ lb firm tofu into large slices, about ¾ inch thick. Use paper towels to dab away excess moisture, then season. Add oil to a large saucepan until it is one-third deep and heat until a piece of bread browns in 15 seconds. Cook the tofu, in batches, for about 3 minutes, until golden all over. Drain on paper towels. Heat a ridged grill pan until smoking and cook the tofu for 1–2 minutes on each side, until charred. Set aside. Toss 2 oz shiitake mushrooms in 2 teaspoons oil and cook on the ridged grill pan until soft, then coarsely chop. Mix the mushrooms with 1 chopped scallion. Use a sharp knife to make a slit in the side of each piece of tofu and stuff it with the mushroom mixture. Mix together 3 tablespoons packed dark brown sugar, 1–2 teaspoons chili sauce, 2 tablespoons tamarind sauce, and 3 tablespoons dark soy sauce. Drizzle the sauce over the tofu pockets to serve.

FOO-VEGE-XYO

Chickpea Falafel Wraps

Serves 4

1 red onion, thinly sliced
2 tablespoons lemon juice
2 (15 oz) cans chickpeas,
  rinsed and drained
2 teaspoons ground cumin
3 scallions, chopped
1 egg, beaten
⅓ cup olive oil
⅓ cup plain yogurt
2 teaspoons tahini
large handful of parsley,
  chopped
2 tomatoes, chopped
salt and black pepper
flatbreads, to serve

- Mix together the onion and lemon juice with some salt and let marinate. Meanwhile, place the chickpeas, cumin, and scallions in a food processor. Season, add 1–2 tablespoons of the egg, and pulse until a chunky paste forms—it should just come together but not be too wet. Shape into walnut-size balls.

- Heat half the oil in a large, nonstick skillet and cook half the falafel for 3–5 minutes, turning once, until golden all over. Set aside on paper towels and cook the remainder in the remaining oil.

- Mix together the yogurt and tahini with a little water to form a thin sauce and season. Toss the marinated onion with the parsley. Arrange the falafels on the flatbreads along with the tomatoes and onion mixture. Drizzle the yogurt sauce over the falafels to serve.

Tomato, Chile, and Chickpea Salad

Rinse and drain 1 (15 oz) can chickpeas. Whisk a good squeeze of lemon juice with ¼ cup olive oil and toss with the chickpeas, 3 chopped tomatoes, and 1 chopped red chile. Season, place in a bowl, and sprinkle with ⅓ cup crumbled feta cheese and a large handful of chopped mint.

Provençal Chickpea Pancake

In a large bowl, mix together 2¾ cups chickpea (besan) flour, a pinch of chili powder, 1¾ cups water, a pinch of salt, and 3 tablespoons olive oil. Let rest for 5 minutes. Whisk 2 egg whites until stiff peaks form, then carefully fold into the batter. Place a 9 inch ovenproof skillet in a preheated oven, at 450°F, and let heat for 5 minutes. Drizzle 2 tablespoons olive oil into the hot skillet, add ½ sliced onion, and swirl around. Pour in the batter and return to the oven for 15 minutes, until just setting. Drizzle 2 tablespoons oil over the pancake and brown under a preheated hot broiler for 1 minute. Top with coarsely chopped tomatoes and serve in wedges.

Butternut Risotto with Chile and Ricotta

Serves 4

4 tablespoons butter
1 tablespoon olive oil
1 onion, finely chopped
2⅓ cups chopped, peeled
  butternut squash
1 red chile, seeded and
  finely chopped
1⅓ cups risotto rice
½ cup dry white wine
3 cups hot vegetable stock
½ cup grated Parmesan cheese
3 sage leaves, finely chopped
¼ cup ricotta cheese
salt and black pepper

- Heat half the butter with the oil in a large saucepan, add the onion, and cook for 5 minutes, until softened. Add the squash and cook for another 2 minutes. Stir most of the chile into the pan along with the rice and cook for 2 minutes, until the rice is well coated.

- Pour the wine into the pan and cook until it has simmered away. Gradually stir in the hot stock, a little at a time, stirring frequently and letting the rice absorb the stock before adding more. When the rice is soft, after about 15 minutes, stir in the remaining butter and the Parmesan and season to taste. Spoon into serving bowls, sprinkle with the sage, ricotta, and remaining chile, and serve.

1 Butternut Chile and Ricotta Gnocchi

Cook 2 cups chopped butternut squash in a large saucepan of lightly salted boiling water for 3 minutes. Add 1 lb fresh gnocchi and cook for 3 minutes or according to the package directions. Drain and toss through 2 finely chopped sage leaves, ½ teaspoon dried red pepper flakes, and 2 tablespoons butter. Season, then spoon onto serving plates and top with dollops of ricotta cheese and some grated Parmesan.

2 Butternut and Ricotta Galette

Peel, seed, and cut ¼ butternut squash into thin slices. Boil together with 1 finely sliced leek for 3 minutes, then drain and cool under cold running water. Mix the leek with ⅓ cup ricotta cheese and season to taste. Unwrap a sheet of ready-to-bake puff pastry on a lightly greased baking sheet. Score a ½ inch border, then spread the leek mixture in the center. Arrange the butternut squash on top and sprinkle with some finely chopped red chile. Brush the pastry border with beaten egg and cook in a preheated oven, at 425°F, for 12–15 minutes, until golden and cooked through.

Crispy Eggplant Slices with Couscous

Serves 4

3 tablespoons all-purpose flour
1 egg, beaten
3 cups dry bread crumbs
1 teaspoon sumac (optional)
finely grated rind and juice of
 1 lemon
2 eggplants, cut into thick slices
⅓ cup vegetable oil
1 cup couscous
1 cup hot vegetable stock
3 tablespoons extra virgin olive oil
¼ cucumber, chopped
1 scallion, chopped
large handful of mint, chopped
large handful of parsley, chopped
salt and black pepper

- Put the flour and egg on separate plates. Mix together the bread crumbs, sumac (if using), and the lemon rind on another plate. Dip the eggplant in the flour and shake to remove any excess. Season well, then dip in the egg and finally in the bread crumb mixture, making sure each slice is well coated.

- Heat half the vegetable oil in a large, nonstick skillet. Add half the eggplants and cook for 3–5 minutes, turning once, until golden and cooked through. Keep warm and repeat with the remaining eggplant and oil.

- Meanwhile, place the couscous in a bowl and pour the stock over the grains. Cover and let sit for 5 minutes, until all the liquid has been absorbed. Pour in the lemon juice and olive oil and let cool a little. Stir through the cucumber, scallion, and herbs and serve alongside the eggplant.

Roasted Eggplant Couscous Salad

Put 1 cup couscous in a bowl and pour 1 cup hot vegetable stock over the grains. Cover the bowl and let sit for 5 minutes, then fluff the couscous up with a fork. Toss with 2 chopped roasted red peppers and 1 chopped roasted eggplant. Add 1 tablespoon lemon juice, 2 tablespoons extra virgin olive oil, a large handful each of mint and parsley leaves, and ½ finely chopped red chile. Season, toss through a handful of arugula leaves, and crumble some goat cheese over the top.

Eggplant and Chickpea Stew with Couscous

Heat 2 tablespoons olive oil in a skillet, add 1 thickly sliced eggplant, and sauté for 3–5 minutes, turning once, until golden. Heat 1 tablespoon olive oil in a large saucepan and cook 1 finely chopped onion for 5 minutes, until softened. Add 2 crushed garlic cloves, 1 teaspoon finely grated fresh ginger root, 1 teaspoon tomato paste, and 1 teaspoon ras el hanout spice mix and cook for 30 seconds. Pour in 1 cup vegetable stock and simmer for 5 minutes. Add the eggplant and cook for another 10 minutes. Rinse and drain 1 (15 oz) can of chickpeas and add to the saucepan with 8 halved cherry tomatoes. Simmer for 2–3 minutes, until the tomatoes are soft and season. Meanwhile, put 1 cup couscous in a bowl, pour 1 cup hot vegetable stock over the grains, and let sit for 5 minutes. Fluff up with a fork, then stir in 2 tablespoons olive oil, 1 tablespoon lemon juice, and a handful of chopped mint. Season and serve the couscous with the stew and some plain yogurt.

Two Bean Chile with Avocado Salsa

Serves 4

2 tablespoons vegetable oil
1 onion, finely chopped
2 garlic cloves, chopped
1 red bell pepper, cored, seeded, and chopped
1 teaspoon ground cumin
½ teaspoon dried oregano
1 (14½ oz) can diced tomatoes
1 (15 oz) can black beans, rinsed and drained
1 cup rinsed and drained, canned kidney beans
1 tablespoon finely chopped semisweet chocolate
salt and black pepper

Salsa

2 avocados, diced
1 scallion, sliced
1 green chile, seeded and chopped
2 tablespoons lime juice
fresh cilantro, chopped

- Heat the oil in a large saucepan, add the onion, and cook for 3 minutes, until starting to soften. Add the garlic and bell pepper and cook for another 3 minutes. Stir in the cumin and oregano, then add the tomatoes, followed by the beans. Let simmer for 10 minutes. Stir in the chocolate until melted and season to taste.

- Toss all the salsa ingredients together. Spoon the chile into serving bowls and top with the salsa.

---

1 Spicy Bean Salad

Rinse and drain 1 (15 oz) can each of pinto and kidney beans. Place in a bowl with 8 halved cherry tomatoes and 2 sliced avocados. Whisk together ¼ cup olive oil, 3 tablespoons lime juice, ½ teaspoon cumin, and ½ chopped red chile. Season, toss with the beans and vegetables, and sprinkle with chopped fresh cilantro.

2 Spicy Beanburgers with Salsa

Rinse and drain 2 (15 oz) cans of kidney beans. Blend the beans in a food processor with ¾ cup fresh bread crumbs, 1 teaspoon ground cumin, and a pinch of chili powder until a coarse paste forms. Season well. Wet your fingers and form the mixture into 4 large patties. Drizzle with 1 tablespoon oil and cook under a preheated hot broiler for 3–5 minutes, until crisp. Turn over and cook for another 3 minutes. Serve in burger buns topped with slices of avocado, a spoonful of tomato salsa, and a dollop of sour cream.

Sweet Potato Soup

Serves 4

1 tablespoon oil
1 tablespoon laksa or
   Thai red curry paste
2 cups vegetable stock
1¾ cups coconut milk
2 lime leaves
2 tablespoons Thai fish sauce
1 large sweet potato,
   peeled and chopped
1 lb rice noodles, cooked
2 cups sugar snap peas
¾ cup bean sprouts
handful of fresh cilantro, chopped
handful of mint leaves, chopped

- Heat the oil in a large saucepan, add the curry paste, and cook for 1 minute, then add the stock, coconut milk, lime leaves, and fish sauce. Bring to a boil, reduce to a simmer, and add the sweet potato. Cook for 12–15 minutes, until soft.

- Add the rice noodles and sugar snap peas and heat through. Ladle into bowls and top with the bean sprouts and herbs.

Grilled Sweet Potato Salad

Thinly slice 2 sweet potatoes and toss in 2 tablespoons oil. Season and cook on a ridged grill pan for 2–3 minutes on each side, until soft and charred. Put ⅓ cup dry shredded coconut in a dry skillet and cook for 1–2 minutes, until lightly browned. Toss the sweet potatoes with 3 tablespoons lime juice, 1 chopped red chile, and plenty of chopped mint and fresh cilantro. Sprinkle with the coconut to serve.

Coconut and Sweet Potato Rice

Heat 2 tablespoons oil in a saucepan, add 1 finely chopped onion, and cook for 5 minutes, until softened. Add 2 chopped sweet potatoes and cook for another 3 minutes. Stir in 2 teaspoons finely grated fresh ginger root and 1 tablespoon Thai red curry paste. Pour in 1½ cups rice and stir around the pan, then add 1¾ cups coconut milk and 1 cup vegetable stock and season to taste. Let simmer for 10 minutes, then add 1 cup sugar snap peas to the pan, cover, and turn the heat to low. Simmer for 5 minutes. Sprinkle with plenty of chopped fresh cilantro and serve.

30 Roasted Pepper and Artichoke Paella

Serves 4

2 tablespoons olive oil
1 onion, finely chopped
2 garlic cloves, chopped
1½ cups paella or risotto rice
1 teaspoon smoked paprika
pinch of dried red pepper flakes
pinch of saffron threads
½ cup dry white wine
1 (14½ oz) can diced tomatoes
1¼ cups vegetable stock
1¼ cups green beans
2 roasted red peppers,
    cut into strips
4 roasted artichoke hearts,
    quartered
handful of parsley, chopped
salt and black pepper
lemon wedges, to serve

- Heat the oil in a deep skillet or paella dish, add the onion, and cook for 5 minutes, until softened. Stir in the garlic and cook for another 1 minute. Add the rice and spices and stir around the skillet until well coated. Pour in the wine and cook until simmered away.

- Add the tomatoes followed by the vegetable stock. Cover and let simmer for 10 minutes. Cook the beans in a saucepan of boiling water for 2 minutes, until starting to soften. Add to the paella along with the roasted peppers and artichokes and cook for another 5 minutes, until the rice is soft. Season to taste, sprinkle with the parsley, and serve with lemon wedges.

---

10 **Artichoke Crostini with Roasted Peppers** Drain 1 (14 oz) can artichokes and pulse in a food processor. Add 3 tablespoons olive oil, 3 tablespoons crème fraîche or sour cream, and 1 tablespoon lemon juice. Season and pulse until almost smooth. Slice a ciabatta loaf and drizzle with oil. Toast under the broiler for 2–3 minutes on each side, then rub with a garlic clove. Spread with the artichoke paste. Top with roasted peppers and arugula.

20 **Artichoke and Roasted Pepper Frittata** Heat 3 tablespoons olive oil in a medium skillet, add 1 chopped onion, and cook for 5 minutes, until softened. Add 1 chopped garlic clove, 4 roasted artichokes hearts, quartered, and 2 roasted red peppers, cut into strips. Cook for 2 minutes. Whisk together 6 eggs with a handful of chopped parsley. Season to taste. Turn the heat to low and pour in the egg mixture.

Cook for 8–10 minutes, until the eggs are just set, finishing under a hot broiler, if needed. Cut into wedges and serve with an arugula salad.

Asparagus Carbonara

Serves 4

1 tablespoon olive oil
2 scallions, chopped
5 oz fine asparagus spears
pinch of chopped tarragon
1 lb fresh linguine
1 egg, lightly beaten
¼ cup crème fraîche or
   heavy cream
½ cup grated Parmesan cheese,
   plus extra to serve
salt and black pepper

- Heat the oil in a large skillet. Add the scallions and asparagus and cook for 2–3 minutes, until just cooked through. Stir in the tarragon.

- Cook the linguine in a large saucepan of lightly salted boiling water according to the package directions. Drain, reserving a little cooking water, and return to the pan. Add the cooked asparagus and onion, then add the egg, crème fraîche, and Parmesan, season, and stir together until creamy, adding a little of the pasta cooking water, if needed. Spoon into bowls and sprinkle with more Parmesan to serve.

Poached Eggs with Asparagus

Toss 5 oz asparagus spears in 2 tablespoons olive oil. Cook on a hot ridged grill pan for 5 minutes, turning frequently, until charred and cooked through. Whisk together 2 tablespoons lemon juice and ¼ cup olive oil, add 1 crushed garlic clove, and season. Cut ½ baguette into small chunks, toss with ⅓ cup olive oil, and bake in a preheated oven, at 400°F, for 7–10 minutes, until golden, then let cool. Poach 4 eggs for 4 minutes for a soft yolk, then pat dry with paper towels. Toss the lemon dressing with 1 (5 oz) package baby spinach leaves and the asparagus. Arrange on plates with the eggs, croutons, and shavings of Parmesan cheese.

Asparagus Tarts

Cook 1 cup asparagus tips in a small saucepan of lightly salted boiling water for 3 minutes or until soft. Drain and cool under cold running water. Meanwhile, melt 4 tablespoons butter in a small saucepan and stir in ¼ cup olive oil. Lightly grease four 5 inch loose-bottom tart pans. Brush 1 sheet of phyllo pastry with the butter mixture. Cut the pastry into 4 squares and arrange these in one of the tart pans. Repeat with the remaining pan. In a small bowl, mix together 5 eggs, ½ cup crème fraîche or heavy cream, a handful of mint leaves, and the finely grated rind of ½ lemon and season well. Spoon the mixture into the tart shells, add the asparagus, and cook in a preheated oven, at 400°F, for 15 minutes or until the pastry is crisp and the filling is just cooked through.

 # Miso Eggplant with Cucumber Rice Noodles

Serves 4

12 baby eggplants, halved
¼ cup white miso paste
3 tablespoons rice wine vinegar
2 tablespoons granulated sugar
1 tablespoon sake or water
1 tablespoon sesame seeds
1 cup edamame (soybeans)
12 oz rice noodles, cooked
½ cucumber, thinly sliced
2 scallions, thinly sliced
salt

- Make a crisscross pattern on the cut sides of the eggplants and place them, cut side down, on a broiler pan. Cook under a preheated hot broiler for 7–10 minutes, until charred. Mix together the miso paste, 2 tablespoons vinegar, the sugar, and sake. Turn the eggplants over and brush with the miso mixture. Return to the broiler for 3–5 minutes, until the eggplant is soft, then sprinkle with the sesame seeds and cook for another 1 minute.

- Meanwhile, cook the edamame in a saucepan of lightly salted boiling water for 2 minutes, until soft. Drain and cool under cold running water. Toss the beans together with the noodles, cucumber, scallions, and the remaining vinegar and season with salt. Serve with the broiled eggplant.

Grilled Eggplant Salad with Miso Ginger Dressing Cut 2 large eggplants into thin slices and toss together with ⅓ cup vegetable oil. Cook on a hot ridged grill pan for 2–3 minutes on each side, until charred and soft. Mix 1 tablespoon white miso paste with 2 tablespoons rice wine vinegar, a pinch of sugar, 2 teaspoons grated fresh ginger root, and ½ finely chopped red chile. Whisk in ⅓ cup vegetable oil, then toss together with the grilled eggplant and 1 (5 oz) package arugula leaves.

 Braised Eggplant and Miso Cut 2 large eggplants into thick chunks. Heat 2 tablespoons vegetable oil in a large saucepan and cook half the eggplant pieces until lightly browned. Remove and repeat with the remaining eggplant. Add a little more oil to the pan, if needed, and cook 1 sliced onion for 5 minutes, until softened. Stir in 2 crushed garlic cloves and 2 teaspoons finely grated fresh ginger root. Cook for 1 minute. Add 1 cup vegetable stock and let simmer for 10 minutes. Add 3 tablespoons white miso paste and 1–2 tablespoons granulated sugar. Return the eggplant to the pan and simmer for 5 minutes, until soft. Cut 2 scallions into thin shreds and sprinkle them over the eggplant before serving with steamed white rice.

 # Leek and Blue Cheese Tart

Serves 4

5 oz baby leeks, trimmed
1 sheet ready-to-bake puff
   pastry
oil, for greasing
1 egg, beaten
⅓ cup mascarpone cheese
1 cup crumbled blue cheese
salt and black pepper

- Cook the leeks in a saucepan of lightly salted boiling water for 1 minute, until just soft. Drain and cool under cold running water.

- Unwrap the pastry onto a lightly greased baking sheet. Use a sharp knife to lightly score a ½ inch border all around the pastry, being careful not to cut all the way through. Lightly mark the inside of the pastry with the end of a fork and brush all over the border with egg.

- Mix together the remaining egg, the mascarpone, and half the blue cheese and spread the mixture over the pastry. Arrange the leeks on top and sprinkle with the remaining cheese. Cook in a preheated oven, at 400°F, for 20 minutes, until the pastry is golden and cooked through.

---

1 Creamy Leek and Blue Cheese Pasta Cut 2 large leeks into thin slices. Cook in a large saucepan of lightly salted boiling water for 3–5 minutes, until soft, together with 1 lb fresh penne, cooked according to the package directions. Drain, reserving a little of the cooking water. Return to the pan and stir in ⅓ cup crème fraîche or sour cream, adding a little of the cooking water, if needed, and sprinkle with 1 cup crumbled blue cheese. Sprinkle with some chopped parsley before serving.

2 Blue Cheese, Cauliflower, and Leek Gratin Melt 2 tablespoons butter in a saucepan, add 3 tablespoons all-purpose flour, and stir together for 1–2 minutes, then slowly whisk in 1¼ cups milk. Cook over low heat, stirring frequently, until the mixture thickens enough to coat the back of a spoon. Take off the heat and add 1¼ cups blue cheese and stir until melted. Meanwhile, cut 1 cauliflower into florets and 2 leeks into thick chunks and cook in a saucepan of lightly salted boiling water for 5–7 minutes, until cooked through. Drain and stir together with the sauce and season to taste. Transfer the mixture to an ovenproof dish and sprinkle with 2 cups dried bread crumbs and a handful of chopped thyme. Place under a medium broiler, drizzle with a little oil, and cook for 5 minutes, until golden and bubbling.

Puffed Goat Cheese and Red Pepper Omelets

Serves 4

6 eggs
¼ cup grated Parmesan cheese
handful of basil, chopped
1 tablespoon olive oil
3 roasted red peppers, sliced
1 cup crumbled soft goat cheese
salt and black pepper

- Crack 3 eggs into a bowl. Separate the remaining 3 eggs and add the yolks to the whole eggs. Stir in the Parmesan and some of the basil and season to taste. Whisk the egg whites until soft peaks form, then carefully fold into the whole egg mixture, one-third at a time.

- Heat the oil in an ovenproof skillet. Add the egg mixture and cook for 2 minutes, then sprinkle with the roasted peppers and goat cheese.

- Place the skillet under a preheated hot broiler and cook for another 5–7 minutes, until puffed and just set. Sprinkle with the remaining basil to serve.

Pecorino Omelets Heat 1 tablespoon butter in a small skillet. Pour in 1 lightly beaten egg and stir around the skillet. Let cook for 30 seconds, until starting to set, then sprinkle with ¼ cup grated Pecorino cheese and add a pinch of dried red pepper flakes. Cook until the omelet is set, then it roll up and keep warm. Make 3 more omelets in the same way. Serve with a green salad.

Red Pepper, Goat Cheese, and Spinach Casserole Heat a large skillet, add 2 tablespoons olive oil and 1 finely chopped onion, and cook for 5 minutes, until softened. Stir in 1 (5 oz) package baby spinach leaves and cook for 1–2 minutes, until wilted. Remove the mixture from the skillet and squeeze away excess water from the spinach. Beat together ⅔ cup ricotta with 6 eggs, then add the spinach mixture, ¼ cup grated Parmesan, and 2 sliced roasted red peppers. Season and pour the mixture into a lightly greased ovenproof dish and sprinkle with ¾ cup crumbled goat cheese. Bake in a preheated oven, at 425°F, for 10–15 minutes, until set, finishing under a hot broiler, if needed.

20 Chargrilled Mozzarella Cheese with Roasted Olives and Salad

Serves 4

3 garlic cloves
⅓ cup olive oil
pinch of dried red pepper flakes
finely grated rind and juice of
  ½ orange
1 teaspoon fennel seeds
1 cup pitted ripe black olives
10 oz new potatoes, halved
1½ cups green beans
8 oz mozzarella or Muenster
  cheese, thickly sliced
1 tablespoon red wine vinegar
8 cherry tomatoes, halved
½ red onion, chopped
handful of oregano leaves,
  chopped
salt and black pepper

- Slice 2 of the garlic cloves and mix together with 2 tablespoons olive oil, the chile, orange rind and juice, fennel seeds, and olives. Place on a small baking sheet and cook in a preheated oven, at 400°F, for 15 minutes.

- Meanwhile, cook the potatoes in a large saucepan of boiling water for 10 minutes, then add the beans and cook for another 3–5 minutes, until soft. Drain and cool under cold running water. Heat a ridged grill pan until smoking. Pat the cheese dry and grill for 2–3 minutes on each side, until golden and lightly charred.

- Crush the remaining garlic and whisk together with the vinegar and the remaining olive oil. Toss the dressing together with the potatoes and beans, tomatoes, and onion. Arrange on a plate with the cheese slices, drizzle with the warm olives and marinade, then sprinkle with the oregano to serve.

---

10 Fried Mozzarella Cheese Sandwich

Cut 8 oz mozarella or Muenster cheese into thick slices. Heat 1 tablespoon olive oil in a nonstick skillet and cook the cheese for 2–3 minutes on each side, until golden. Add 1 tablespoon capers and remove from the heat. Halve 4 small baguettes. Chop 1 Boston lettuce and 4 cherry tomatoes and place on top. Sprinkle with ½ cup pitted ripe black olives, drizzle with 2 tablespoons lemon juice, and top with the cheese and capers.

30 Cheese-Topped Stuffed Red Peppers

Core, seed, and halve 2 red bell peppers. Halve 4 plum tomatoes and put them with the bell peppers on a lightly greased baking sheet. Mix together 2 teaspoons red wine vinegar, a pinch of sugar, and 1 tablespoon olive oil, drizzle the dressing over the bell peppers and tomatoes and cook in a preheated oven, at 375°F, for 10 minutes. Add 1¼ cups pitted olives, the finely grated rind of 1 orange, a pinch of dried red pepper flakes, and some chopped oregano leaves. Season, drizzle with 2 tablespoons olive oil, and cook for another 15 minutes. Coarsely chop the tomatoes and olives and toss through 2 teaspoons capers and a large handful each of chopped mint and dill. Fill the bell pepper halves with the tomato mixture. Cut 8 oz mozzarella or Muenster cheese into thin slices, top the bell peppers with the cheese, and cook under a hot broiler until browned. Serve with lettuce.

Puttanesca Pizza

Serves 4

2 (6½ oz) packages pizza
   crust mix
1 tablespoon olive oil, plus extra
   for greasing
1 cup prepared tomato sauce
8 cherry tomatoes, halved
1 red chile, seeded and sliced
4 oz mozzarella cheese, sliced
½ cup pitted olives
1 tablespoon capers
handful of arugula leaves,
   to serve

- Mix the pizza crust according to the package directions and knead for 3 minutes. Roll out the dough into an oval shape, about 10 inches long, and place on a lightly greased baking sheet. Spread over the tomato sauce and let rise for 5–10 minutes. Arrange the halved tomatoes, chile, mozzarella, olives, and capers on top. Drizzle over the oil.

- Bake in a preheated oven, at 425°F, for 15 minutes, until the pizza is crisp. Top with the arugula leaves before serving.

1 **Pasta Puttanesca**
Cook 1 lb fresh penne pasta in a large saucepan of lightly salted boiling water according to the package directions. Drain and toss through 3 chopped tomatoes, 1 tablespoon capers, ½ cup pitted olives, 1 tablespoon lemon juice, ¼ cup olive oil, and a handful of chopped parsley. Season and serve immediately.

2 **Skillet Pizza with Puttanesca**
Topping Mix 2 (6½ oz) packages pizza crust mix according to the package directions and knead for 3 minutes. Divide into 2 balls and roll each into a circle 9 inches across. Heat 1 tablespoon olive oil in a large skillet, add a pizza crust, and cook for 5 minutes, until golden. Turn over and cook for another 3 minutes, until cooked through. Repeat with the remaining crust. Spread 1 cup prepared tomato sauce over each pizza and top with 5 oz sliced mozzarella. Cook under a hot broiler for 1–2 minutes, until melted, then sprinkle with 2 tablespoons drained capers, ½ cup pitted olives, and a handful of arugula to serve.

Carrot and Beet Tabbouleh

Serves 4

1 cup bulgur wheat
1 garlic clove, crushed
pinch of ground cinnamon
pinch of allspice
2 tablespoons pomegranate
    molasses or pomegranate juice
⅓ cup extra virgin olive oil
1 carrot, grated
2 cooked beets, cubed
2 scallions, sliced
½ green chile, chopped
large handful of mint, chopped
large handful of parsley, chopped
⅓ cup crumbled feta cheese
salt and black pepper

- Prepare the bulgur wheat according to the package directions, then drain thoroughly.

- Mix together the garlic, spices, pomegranate molasses, and olive oil. Toss together with the bulgur wheat, carrot, beets, scallions, chile, mint, and parsley and season to taste. Sprinkle with the feta to serve.

---

20 **Spicy Carrot Stew with Couscous**

Cook 1 sliced onion, 1 sliced parsnip, and 2 sliced carrots in 1 tablespoon oil for 7 minutes until soft. Stir in 2 teaspoons ras el hanout spice mix and 2 crushed garlic cloves. Pour in 1¼ cups vegetable stock and simmer for 10 minutes. Add 1 cup cooked chickpeas and a little lemon juice and heat through. Meanwhile, pour 1½ cups hot stock over 1¾ cups couscous, cover, and let sit for 5 minutes. Stir through ¼ cup toasted slivered almonds, 1 sliced scallion, and a handful each of chopped mint and parsley.

30 **Warm Roasted Carrot and Beet Tabbouleh** Put 3 halved small carrots on a large piece of aluminum foil. Drizzle with 2 tablespoons olive oil, then fold the foil to loosely enclose. Place on a baking sheet and cook in a preheated oven, at 400°F, for 20–25 minutes, until soft. Wrap 2 roasted beets, cut into thick slices, in some foil and cook for the last 5 minutes of cooking time to heat through. Heat 2 tablespoons olive oil in a saucepan, add 1 sliced onion, and cook for 10 minutes, until golden and soft. Add 1½ cups

bulgur wheat and pour 1 cup boiling vegetable stock over the grains. Cover and let simmer for 5–10 minutes, until soft. Use a fork to fluff through, then stir in 1 tablespoon lemon juice and another 2 tablespoons olive oil. Toss through the roasted vegetables and 3½ cups arugula leaves, season to taste, and sprinkle with ⅓ cup goat cheese to serve.

Roasted Cauliflower with Tomato Sauce

Serves 4

1 cauliflower, separated
  into florets
3 tablespoons oil
1 teaspoon cumin seeds
1 lemon, cut into wedges
1 onion, finely chopped
1 tablespoon rogan josh
  curry paste
1 (14½ oz) can diced tomatoes
¼ cup cashew nuts
handful of fresh cilantro, chopped
salt and black pepper
boiled rice, to serve

- Put the cauliflower in a roasting pan and toss together with 2 tablespoons oil, the cumin seeds, and lemon. Bake in a preheated oven, at 425°F, for 20–25 minutes, until soft and lightly charred.

- Meanwhile, heat the remaining oil in a saucepan, add the onion, and cook for 5 minutes, until softened. Stir in the curry paste and cook for 1 minute. Pour in the tomatoes and let simmer for 15 minutes. Season to taste.

- Heat a dry skillet and cook the cashew nuts until golden, then set aside to cool. Squeeze a couple of lemon wedges over the roasted cauliflower and pile on a plate. Spoon the tomato sauce over the cauliflower, sprinkle with the cashew nuts and fresh cilantro, and serve with plain boiled rice.

Spicy Cauliflower and Tomato Cheese

Separate a cauliflower into florets and cook in a large saucepan of lightly salted boiling water for 7 minutes, until soft. Drain, reserving ¼ cup cooking water. Stir the water with ⅔ cup crème fraîche or heavy cream and 1 teaspoon garam masala, and toss with the cauliflower. Place in an ovenproof dish. Arrange 1 sliced tomato on top, then cook under a hot preheated broiler for 1–2 minutes, until lightly browned and bubbling.

Cauliflower and Tomato Curry

Heat 1 tablespoon oil in a large saucepan, add 1 finely chopped onion, and cook for 5 minutes, until softened. Stir in 2 finely chopped garlic cloves and 2 teaspoons grated fresh ginger root. Add 1 teaspoon each ground cumin and ground coriander, ½ teaspoon ground turmeric, and a pinch of cayenne pepper. Pour in 1 (14½ oz) can diced tomatoes and season to taste. Break 1 cauliflower into florets and add to the pan. Let simmer for 12–15 minutes, until the cauliflower is soft. Drizzle with a little plain yogurt and chopped fresh cilantro and serve with some warm naan.

Eggplant Caponata with Ricotta

Serves 4

⅓ cup olive oil
1 onion, sliced
2 celery sticks, sliced
1 garlic clove, sliced
2 teaspoons tomato paste
1 (14½ oz) can plum tomatoes
2 eggplants, cubed
2 tablespoons white wine vinegar
2 teaspoons granulated sugar
1 tablespoon capers, rinsed
1¼ cups large green olives
½ cup ricotta cheese
¼ cup toasted pine nuts
handful of basil, chopped
salt and black pepper

- Heat 1 tablespoon olive oil in a large saucepan, add the onion and celery, and cook for 5 minutes, until softened. Add the garlic and tomato paste and cook for another 1 minute. Add the tomatoes, top up with a little water, and let simmer for 5 minutes.

- Meanwhile, heat half the remaining oil in a skillet, add half the eggplant, and cook for 5 minutes, turning occasionally, until browned. Remove from the skillet with a slotted spoon and let drain on paper towels. Repeat with the remaining oil and eggplant.

- Stir the vinegar and sugar into the tomato sauce, and add the cooked eggplant, capers, and olives. Season to taste and let simmer for 7–10 minutes. Spoon into serving bowls, top with a dollop of the ricotta, and sprinkle with pine nuts and basil before serving.

---

1 Grilled Eggplant Salad with Honey and Vinegar Cut 2 eggplants into thin slices and toss with ⅓ cup olive oil. Season well and cook in a hot ridged grill pan for 2 minutes on each side, until soft and charred. Drizzle with 1 teaspoon honey, 1 tablespoon sherry vinegar, and 3 tablespoons extra virgin olive oil. Sprinkle with 1 sliced roasted red pepper, 1 seeded and chopped chile, and a handful of chopped mint leaves. Serve with a mixed tomato and arugula salad.

3 Roasted Eggplant and Red Peppers with Tahini Dressing Slice 1 large eggplant, 1 large zucchini, 2 red bell peppers, and 1 onion and toss together with ¼ cup olive oil, 1 tablespoon balsamic vinegar, 2 teaspoons packed light brown sugar, and 2 teaspoons harissa until well coated. Place the vegetable mixture on a baking sheet, season, and roast in a preheated oven, at 425°F, for 25 minutes, turning occasionally, until charred and soft. Stir through 2 tablespoons raisins. Meanwhile, mix ⅓ cup plain yogurt with 3 tablespoons tahini, 1 crushed garlic clove, and 1 tablespoon lemon juice. Stir in a handful of chopped fresh cilantro and drizzle the dressing over the vegetables before serving.

Spicy Grilled Zucchini with Mashed Chickpeas

Serves 4

2 (15 oz) cans chickpeas,
   rinsed and drained
1 garlic clove, crushed
1 teaspoon ground cumin
1 tablespoon tahini
3 tablespoons lemon juice
½ cup olive oil
8 baby zucchini, halved
finely grated rind of ½ lemon
1 tablespoon harissa
2 teaspoons tomato paste
handful of mint leaves
salt and black pepper
lightly toasted pita bread,
   to serve

- Warm the chickpeas in a large saucepan of boiling water for 1 minute and drain, reserving a little of the water. Return to the pan, reserving a few whole chickpeas. Add ¼ cup of the cooking water (or more, if needed), the garlic, cumin, tahini, 2 tablespoons lemon juice, and ¼ cup olive oil and blend with an immersion blender or in a food processor until a chunky puree forms. Season to taste and keep warm.

- Meanwhile, toss the zucchini with 1 tablespoon oil, season well, and cook on a ridged grill pan for 2–3 minutes on each side, until soft and lightly charred. Mix together the remaining oil and lemon juice, the lemon rind, harissa, and the tomato paste. Arrange the mashed chickpea and zucchini on plates and sprinkle the reserved chickpeas over the mashed chickpeas. Drizzle with the dressing and sprinkle with mint leaves before serving with pita bread.

Vegetable and Chickpea Stew

Cook 1 chopped onion in 2 tablespoons oil for 5 minutes, until softened. Stir in 1 crushed garlic clove, 2 teaspoons ground cumin, 1 teaspoon grated fresh ginger root, and a pinch of ground cinnamon. Add 1 (14½ oz) can diced tomatoes and simmer for 5 minutes. Meanwhile, in batches, sauté 1 sliced zucchini, 1 eggplant, cut into chunks, and 1 red bell pepper, cut into chunks, until soft and lightly charred. Stir into the sauce with 1 cup rinsed and drained, canned chickpeas. Simmer for 5–10 minutes. Drizzle with plain yogurt and sprinkle with fresh cilantro to serve.

Chickpea Pilaf with Zucchini Curls

Heat 3 tablespoons olive oil in a large saucepan, add 1 finely chopped onion, and cook for 5 minutes, until softened. Stir in 2 crushed garlic cloves and cook for 30 seconds. Add 1¼ cups long grain rice and stir around the pan, then pour in 3 cups vegetable stock. Bring to a boil and let simmer for about 10 minutes, until most of the liquid has simmered away. Add 1 (15 oz) can rinsed and drained chickpeas. Turn the heat to very low, cover with a lid, and let steam for 5 minutes, until the rice is soft. Meanwhile, use a vegetable peeler to slice off thin curls from 2 large zucchini. Just before serving, toss with 2 tablespoons extra virgin olive oil and 1 tablespoon lemon juice and season well. Pile the rice onto plates and top with the zucchini curls. Sprinkle with ½ cup crumbled feta cheese before serving.

Mushroom Risotto with Gremolata

Serves 4

1 tablespoon olive oil
4 tablespoons butter
8 oz wild mushrooms,
  halved if large
1 onion, finely chopped
1½ cups risotto rice
½ cup dry white wine
3¾ cups hot vegetable stock
¼ cup grated Parmesan cheese
2 garlic cloves, finely chopped
finely grated rind of 1 lemon
large handful of parsley, chopped
salt and black pepper

- Heat the oil and half the butter in a large, deep skillet, add the mushrooms, and cook for 2–3 minutes, until lightly browned. Set aside. Add the onion to the skillet and cook for 5 minutes, until softened, then stir in the rice and cook for 2 minutes, until the rice is well coated.

- Pour the wine into the skillet and cook until it has simmered away. Gradually stir in the hot stock, a little at a time, stirring frequently and letting the rice absorb the stock before adding more. When the rice is soft, after about 15 minutes, stir in the remaining butter, the mushrooms, and the Parmesan.

- Meanwhile, mix together the garlic, grated lemon rind, and parsley. Spoon the risotto into serving bowls and sprinkle with the gremolata.

---

1 **Warm Mushroom and Spicy Gremolata Salad** Put 12 medium portabello mushrooms on a lightly greased baking sheet. Mix the finely grated rind of 1 lemon, 2 tablespoons lemon juice, 1 crushed garlic clove, a handful of chopped parsley, and ½ finely chopped chile with ⅓ cup olive oil. Drizzle the mixture over the mushrooms and season to taste. Cook in a preheated oven, at 425°F, for 8 minutes, until lightly charred. Toss 1 (7 oz) package mixed salad greens with 2 tablespoons lemon juice and some olive oil. Serve with the mushrooms and some roasted red peppers.

2 **Creamy Mushroom Soup with Gremolata Drizzle** Heat 2 tablespoons butter in a large saucepan, add 10 oz mushrooms, and cook for 2–3 minutes, until lightly browned. Remove from the pan. Add 1 finely chopped onion and cook for 2 minutes, then stir in 1 oz dried porcini mushrooms. Pour in 5 cups vegetable stock, add a sprig of rosemary, and let simmer for 10 minutes. Return half the mushrooms to the pan along with ⅓ cup heavy cream and season to taste. Blend with an immersion blender until smooth, then add the remaining mushrooms. Mix together

3 tablespoons olive oil, 1 crushed garlic clove, the finely grated rind of 1 lemon, and a handful each of chopped parsley and basil leaves. Swirl the mixture over the soup before serving.

Eggplant, Tomato, and Mozzarella Melts

Serves 4

5 tablespoons olive oil
12 baby eggplants, halved
½ cup tomato puree or sauce
4 cherry tomatoes, chopped
pinch of dried red pepper flakes
handful of oregano leaves,
   chopped
7 oz mozzarella, sliced
salt and black pepper

- Rub the oil over the eggplants and season well. Place them under a hot broiler and cook for 5–7 minutes on each side or until soft and golden brown.

- Mix together the tomato puree, tomatoes, red pepper flakes, and oregano and season well. Arrange the eggplants, cut side up, in the broiler pan, spoon a little of the tomato mixture on top of each eggplant, and place some mozzarella slices on top. Return to the broiler and cook for 2–3 minutes, until the mozzarella has just melted.

10 Eggplant Baguette Melts

Arrange 8 thick slices of roasted eggplant in a broiler pan. Coarsely chop 2 large tomatoes and sprinkle them on top together with 4 oz torn mozzarella. Cook under a hot broiler for 2 minutes, until the cheese melts. Lightly toast 4 individual baguettes. Place the eggplants inside together with a large handful of arugula leaves.

30 Eggplant, Mozzarella, and Pesto Gratin

Slice 4 large eggplants into ½ inch strips. Heat 2 tablespoons olive oil in a large skillet and cook the strips in batches, adding more oil, if needed, for 2–3 minutes on each side, until golden and soft. Arrange half the eggplants in a medium gratin dish. Spoon ½ cup tomator puree or sauce mixed with a pinch of dried red pepper flakes over the eggplants, followed by 3 oz mozzarella cut into slices. Drizzle with ¼ cup fresh green pesto. Top with a second layer of eggplant, then another ½ cup tomato puree or sauce. Arrange 4 oz mozzarella on top and sprinkle with ½ cup grated Parmesan. Cook in a preheated oven, at 400°F, for 15–20 minutes, until golden and bubbling.

30 Broccoli, Blue Cheese, and Walnut Pie

Serves 4

6 cups broccoli florets
1 bunch watercress or
  1 (5 oz) package arugula
⅔ cup mascarpone cheese
2 eggs plus 1 egg yolk,
  lightly beaten
1¼ cup crumbled blue cheese
2 tablespoons butter, melted
¼ cup olive oil
5 large sheets phyllo pastry
¼ cup coarsely chopped walnuts
salt and black pepper

- Cook the broccoli in a large saucepan of boiling salted water for 2 minutes, until just soft. Drain and cool under cold running water. Place the watercress in a strainer and pour boiling water over the leaves until wilted, then squeeze away excess water.

- Mix together the mascarpone and eggs and season with salt and black pepper. Add the broccoli, watercress, and blue cheese. Mix together the butter and oil and brush around an 8 inch springform cake pan. Brush over a sheet of phyllo pastry, keeping the remainder of the pastry covered with damp, but not wet, paper towels. Put the pastry in the cake pan, letting the excess hang over the sides. Turn the pan and place another sheet, brushed with the butter mixture, on top. Repeat until the pan is lined and the pastry used up.

- Spoon the filling into the pan and pull the overhanging pastry over to cover, scrunching the corners up a little as you work. Brush with more of the butter mixture, then sprinkle with the walnuts. Bake in a preheated oven, at 400°F, for 20–25 minutes, until golden and crispy.

---

10 Broccoli Blue Cheese Gratin

Boil 6 cups broccoli florets for 4 minutes or until soft and drain. Mix together 1 cup crème fraîche or heavy cream, 1 cup blue cheese, and 3 tablespoons milk, stir through the broccoli, and heat through. Place in an ovenproof dish and sprinkle with 1 cup dried bread crumbs and ¼ cup chopped walnuts, then drizzle with 1 tablespoon oil. Cook under a hot broiler for 2 minutes, until golden and crisp.

20 Broccoli Soup with Melting Blue Cheese Bites

Heat 1 tablespoon oil in a large saucepan, add 1 finely chopped onion, and cook for 5 minutes, until softened. Add 6 cups broccoli florets and pour in 5 cups vegetable stock. Let simmer for 7–10 minutes, until the broccoli is really soft. Stir in 3 tablespoons crème fraîche or sour cream, season to taste, and use an immersion blender to blend to a smooth puree.

Meanwhile, slice 1 small baguette. Under a hot broiler, toast the baguette slices on one side for 1 minute, until golden and crisp, then turn over and broil for another 1 minute. Mix together 1¼ cups crumbled blue cheese and ¼ cup crème fraîche or sour cream. Spread this mixture over the baguette slices and sprinkle with a handful of chopped walnuts. Return to the broiler for 2 minutes, until bubbling and melted and serve alongside the soup.

Polenta Wedges with Onion Marmalade and Goat Cheese

Serves 4

4 cups hot vegetable stock
2 cups instant polenta
3 tablespoons olive oil
handful of arugula leaves
1¼ cups crumbled soft
  goat cheese
¼ cup walnuts, toasted
⅓ cup onion marmalade or relish
salt and black pepper

· Put the stock in a large saucepan, add the polenta, and stir vigorously. Cook for 5 minutes, until thickened and season to taste. Line a 9 inch springform cake pan with a circle of parchment paper and grease the sides. Pour in the polenta. Place in the freezer for 10 minutes, until cold and solid.

· Remove the polenta from the pan and cut into wedges. Brush over the wedges with 2 tablespoons olive oil, place under a preheated hot broiler, and cook for 2–3 minutes on each side, until golden.

· Transfer to serving plates and sprinkle with the arugula leaves and walnuts. Sprinkle with the crumbled goat cheese, drizzle with the remaining olive oil, and spoon some marmalade onto each plate.

---

1 **Goat Cheese and Onion Marmalade Crostini** Cut ½ ciabatta loaf into slices. Drizzle with olive oil, then toast under a hot broiler for 2–3 minutes on each side, until golden. Spread each slice with 1 heaping teaspoon onion marmalade or relish and top with a slice of goat cheese. Put under a hot broiler for 1 minute, until melting, then sprinkle with chopped chives to serve.

3 **Polenta Wedges with Caramelized Onions** Prepare the polenta wedges as above. Meanwhile, heat 1 tablespoon oil in a large skillet set over low heat, add 2 sliced red onions, and cook for 20 minutes, until browned and caramelized. Add ½ cup firmly packed light brown sugar, ½ cup red wine vinegar, and 2–3 tablespoons balsamic vinegar. Increase the heat and cook for 7–10 minutes, until all the liquid has been absorbed. Serve the polenta with the onions on the side.

QuickCook
Desserts

Recipes listed by cooking time

30

2

Strawberry Meringue Roulade

Serves 6

4 egg whites
1 cup granulated sugar
1 teaspoon vanilla extract
1¼ cups heavy cream
⅓ cup confectioners' sugar,
  plus extra for dusting
3 tablespoons strawberry jam
  or preserves
¾ cup sliced strawberries

- Line a 12 × 8 inch jelly roll pan with parchment paper. Whip the egg whites until stiff peaks appear, then add the sugar, a tablespoon at a time, and keep whisking until you have a stiff, glossy meringue. Stir through the vanilla extract.

- Spoon the batter into the pan and smooth over the surface. Place in a preheated oven, at 400°F, and immediately reduce the temperature to 325°F. Cook for 15 minutes, until firm to the touch.

- Turn the meringue out onto a sheet of parchment paper dusted with confectioners' sugar and let cool for 3 minutes. Peel off the lining paper from the top of the meringue, then carefully roll up the meringue from the long side. Set aside to cool.

- Whip the heavy cream with the confectioners' sugar, unroll the meringue, and spread the cream on top. Mix the jam with a splash of boiling water to loosen, then spoon it over the cream and top with the sliced strawberries. Using the parchment paper, roll up the meringue and place on a serving plate. Dust with some more confectioners' sugar and serve.

1 Strawberry and Meringue Desserts

Whip 2½ cups heavy cream until soft peaks form. Stir in 1 teaspoon vanilla extract and 3–4 tablespoons confectioners' sugar. Crush 4 prepared small meringues and place in the bottom of 6 serving glasses. Stir 1⅓ cups sliced strawberries through the cream. Spoon the cream over the meringue and top with sliced strawberries.

2 Strawberry Meringue Tarts

Spread 1 heaping tablespoon strawberry jam or preserves in each of 6 individual tart shells. Whip 3 egg whites until stiff peaks form. Then, a tablespoon at a time, whip in ½ cup granulated sugar until glossy and thick. Swirl the mixture over the jam. Cook in a preheated oven, at 400°F, for 5–7 minutes, until the meringue is golden.

 # Molten Chocolate Cakes

Serves 4

1 stick butter, plus extra
for greasing
4 oz semisweet chocolate,
chopped
2 eggs
2 egg yolks
¼ cup sugar
2 teaspoons flour, plus extra
for dusting
confectioners' sugar, for dusting

- Butter and lightly flour 4 oven-proof teacups or dariole molds. Put the butter and chocolate in a bowl set over a saucepan of simmering water, being careful that the bottom of the bowl does not touch the water, until the chocolate melts (or use a double boiler). Let cool a little.

- Use a handheld electric mixer to beat the eggs, egg yolks, and sugar until light and thick. Pour the melted chocolate mixture into the eggs, then quickly stir in with the flour until just combined.

- Spoon the batter into the molds and bake in a preheated oven, at 450°F, for 6–7 minutes; the sides should be just set but the centers still soft. Let rest for a moment, then serve in the teacups, dusted with confectioners' sugar, or invert each cake onto a plate, lift away the molds, and dust with confectioners' sugar.

---

1 Chocolate Soufflé Wraps

Whisk 4 egg whites until stiff peaks form. Stir in 4 lightly beaten egg yolks, 1 teaspoon vanilla extract, and 3 oz grated semisweet chocolate. Heat 1 tablespoon butter in a small nonstick skillet, add one-quarter of the egg mixture, and cook for 1 minute, until nearly set. Spread some prepared chocolate sauce on the omelet and fold up. Repeat with the remaining mixture to make 4 wraps and serve with mixed berries.

3 Chocolate Soufflés

Melt 6 oz semisweet chocolate in bowl set over a saucepan of simmering water (or use a double boiler). Let cool. Grease 4 individual ramekins with a little butter, then swirl 1 tablespoon sugar around each to coat. Beat 4 egg whites until stiff, then carefully whisk in ¼ cup sugar until stiff and glossy. Stir 4 egg yolks into the cooled chocolate. Stir one-third of the whites into the chocolate, then gently fold in the remaining whites, half at a time, until just combined. Spoon the chocolate mixture into the molds and rub your thumb around the inside of each. Bake in a preheated oven, at 400°F, for 10–12 minutes, until puffed.

 # Vanilla Baked Apricots with Ricotta Cream

Serves 4

10 apricots, halved and pitted

1 cup white wine

1 teaspoon vanilla extract

²⁄₃ cup granulated sugar

1 cup ricotta

3 tablespoons heavy cream

2 tablespoons confectioners' sugar

- Arrange the apricots, cut side up, in a single layer in an ovenproof dish. Heat the wine in a small saucepan. Add the vanilla extract and sugar to the pan and stir together until the sugar dissolves. Pour the liquid over the apricots and bake in a preheated oven, at 375°F, for 15 minutes or until the apricots are soft and a little browned. Let cool slightly.

- Put the ricotta, cream, and confectioners' sugar in a food processor and pulse until smooth. Spoon the apricots into bowls with the juices and top with the ricotta mixture to serve.

---

1 **Apricot Ricotta Desserts**

Blend 1 cup ricotta and ²⁄₃ cup store-bought vanilla pudding in a food processor until smooth. Sprinkle 2 cups crushed amaretti or shortbread cookies into serving bowls, reserving a few crumbs. Drizzle with 2 tablespoons Amaretto liqueur or 1 tablespoon orange juice and add 4 pitted and chopped apricots. Spoon the ricotta mixture over the top and sprinkle with extra cookie crumbs.

2 **Ricotta Hot Cakes with Apricots**

Place 1²⁄₃ cups all-purpose flour in a bowl with 1 teaspoon baking powder. Stir in 1 egg, then slowly whisk in 1 cup milk and 1 teaspoon vanilla extract until combined. Stir in ¾ cup ricotta; don't worry if there are still some lumps of ricotta. Heat a large nonstick skillet, add 1 teaspoon oil and 1 tablespoon butter, and melt. Add spoonfuls of the ricotta mixture and cook for 2–3 minutes on each side, until golden and just cooked through. Remove from skillet and keep warm. Repeat with the remaining mixture. Pile up onto plates and spoon store-bought apricot compote or preserves over the top to serve.

 # Coffee Cocktail with Almond Cookies

Serves 4

1¾ cups ground almonds
  (almond meal)
1 cup granulated sugar
½ teaspoon baking powder
1 egg white, lightly beaten
confectioners' sugar, for dusting

For the cocktail

½ cup strong coffee, cooled
¼ cup coffee liqueur
¼–⅓ cup heavy cream

- Line a baking sheet with parchment paper. Put the almonds, sugar, and baking powder in a bowl and stir through the beaten egg white to make a soft paste. Knead briefly, then roll into a long cylinder. Slice off ½ inch pieces and lightly pinch each end to make oval shapes. Place on the baking sheet and bake in a preheated oven, at 400°F, for 10 minutes or until pale golden. Let cool and dust with plenty of confectioners' sugar.

- Meanwhile, make the cocktail. Mix together the coffee and coffee liqueur and pour into 4 martini glasses. Slowly pour in the cream over the back of a teaspoon so it settles on the top. Serve with the cookies.

1 **Creamy Irish Coffee**

Place 1 tablespoon whiskey and 1 tablespoon granulated sugar into each of 4 serving glasses. Pour in hot strong coffee and stir together. Lightly whisk ½ cup heavy cream with 3 tablespoons Irish cream liqueur. Spoon the cream mixture over the coffee and serve with some chocolate-coated almonds.

3 **Chocolate Coffee Cream**

Bring 1¼ cups heavy cream to a boil in a small saucepan. Pour in 3 tablespoons Kahlua, then add 4 oz chopped semisweet chocolate and stir until smooth. Divide among 4 serving bowls and place in the freezer for 20 minutes or until set. Spoon ½ cup heavy cream whipped with 1 tablespoon confectioners' sugar over the top. Serve with almond cookies.

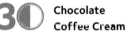

FOO-PUDD-RUK

 # Iced Berries with White Chocolate Sauce

Serves 4

¾ cup heavy cream
6 oz white chocolate, chopped
½ teaspoon vanilla extract
4 cups mixed frozen berries

- Put the cream in a small saucepan and heat until boiling. Take off the heat and stir in the chocolate and vanilla extract and mix until melted.

- Arrange the berries in chilled serving bowls, drizzle with the sauce, and serve.

2 White Chocolate Berry Mousses

Melt 6 oz white chocolate in a bowl over a saucepan of simmering water (or in a double boiler) and let cool a little. Beat 1 cup cream cheese and mix in 1 cup heavy cream until smooth. Stir in the cooled chocolate. In a separate bowl, whisk 3 eggs with ⅔ cup granulated sugar until light and fluffy. Fold into the cream cheese mixture, one-third at a time. Place a handful of mixed berries in 4 serving dishes and spoon some of the cream mixture on top, followed by some more berries. Keep layering and finish with shavings of white chocolate.

3 White Chocolate and Berry Cookies

Melt 3 oz white chocolate in a bowl over a saucepan of simmering water (or in a double boiler). Let cool a little. Beat 1 stick butter and ½ cup granulated sugar until fluffy, then beat in 1 egg and 1 teaspoon vanilla extract. Add 1 teaspoon baking powder and 1⅓ cups all-purpose flour and stir together. Add 4 oz chopped white chocolate and 1 cup dried mixed berries. Roll into small, walnut-size balls and place on a baking sheet lined with parchment paper. Bake in a preheated oven, at 350°F, for 12–15 minutes, until golden. Let cool for 1 minute, then serve.

Warm Almond Cakes with Fig Compote

Serves 6

1⅓ cups confectioners' sugar, sifted

¾ cup ground almonds (almond meal)

⅓ cup all-purpose flour

4 egg whites

1 stick butter, melted, plus extra for greasing

¼ cup slivered almonds

8 figs, quartered

½ cup port

1 tablespoon packed light brown sugar

strip of orange rind

crème fraîche or whipped cream, to serve

- Grease and flour a 12-cup cupcake or madeleine pan. Place the confectioners' sugar, ground almonds, and flour in a mixing bowl. Stir in the egg whites until well combined, then beat in the melted butter until smooth. Spoon the batter into the pan and sprinkle a few slivered almonds on top of each cake. Bake in a preheated oven, at 400°F, for 12–15 minutes, until golden.

- To make the compote, put the figs, port, and sugar in a small saucepan with the orange rind and cook for 5–10 minutes, until soft and syrupy. Let cool a little. Spoon some of the compote over the cakes and serve with a spoonful of crème fraîche.

1 Fig and Almond Trifles

Slice 4 oz of store-bought pound cake into small cubes and place in the bottom of 4 serving bowls. Sprinkle with 2 tablespoons orange juice and 2 tablespoons port. Coarsely chop 8 figs and place on top. Whip ⅔ cup heavy cream with 1 tablespoon confectioners' sugar until soft peaks form. Spoon 1 cup store-bought vanilla pudding into the bowls. Top with the cream and sprinkle with ¼ cup toasted slivered almonds to serve.

2 Baked Figs with Almond Cookies

Halve 8 figs and place in an ovenproof dish. Dot with 2 tablespoons butter and sprinkle with 2 tablespoons packed light brown sugar. Pour in ¼ cup orange juice and 3 tablespoons port, then bake in a preheated oven, at 400°F, for 15 minutes, until soft. Spoon vanilla ice cream over the top and serve with crisp almond cookies.

 # Cinnamon Plum Crisp

Serves 4

10 plums, pitted and sliced
4 teaspoons granulated sugar
juice of 1 orange
1 stick butter
1¼ cups all-purpose flour
1 teaspoon ground cinnamon
¼ cup firmly packed light
 brown sugar
½ cup chopped hazelnuts
custard or cream, to serve

- Put the plums, granulated sugar, and orange juice in a saucepan and cook for 3 minutes or until starting to soften, then spoon into an ovenproof dish. Melt the butter and mix together with the remaining ingredients. Crumble the mixture over the plums, breaking up any large clumps.

- Bake in a preheated oven, at 375°F, for 20–25 minutes, until the topping is crisp. Serve with plenty of custard.

1 Prune, Port, and Cinnamon Whips

In a small food processor, blend together ¾ cup soft pitted prunes (dried plums) with a pinch of ground cinnamon and ¼ cup port to make a smooth paste. Whisk 1 cup heavy cream until soft peaks form, then swirl in the prune mixture. Place in 4 serving glasses and crumble 2 gingersnap cookies on top.

2 Baked Cinnamon Plums

Place 8 pitted and halved plums on a baking sheet. Rub 4 tablespoons chilled butter, cut into cubes, into 3 tablespoons packed light brown sugar, ½ teaspoon ground cinnamon, and ⅔ cup all-purpose flour. Sprinkle this mixture over the plums, then bake in a preheated oven, at 400°F, for 15 minutes or until soft and lightly browned.

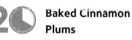

 # Date Cakes with Caramel Sauce

Serves 4

⅔ cup pitted dates
½ cup water
1 teaspoon baking soda
4 tablespoons butter, softened,
  plus extra for greasing
⅓ cup firmly packed light
  brown sugar
1 egg
1 tablespoon light corn syrup
½ teaspoon vanilla extract
¾ cup all-purpose flour

For the sauce

¼ cup firmly packed dark
  brown sugar
4 tablespoons butter
⅓ cup heavy cream

- Grease 4 individual bundt pans or dessert molds. Put the dates and water in a small saucepan, bring to a boil, and simmer for 3 minutes. Remove from the heat and add the baking soda (which will froth up). Place in the freezer to cool a little.

- Blend together the remaining ingredients in a food processor. Add the cooled dates with the cooking liquid and process until smooth.

- Spoon the batter into the pans and cook in a preheated oven, at 375°F, for 20–25 minutes, until just cooked through.

- Meanwhile, make the sauce by placing all the ingredients in a small saucepan over low heat. Stir together until smooth and the butter has melted, then keep warm. Turn the cakes out from their molds, spoon some sauce over them, and serve the rest in a small pitcher.

---

1 **Date and Caramel Sundaes**

Heat 10 chopped pitted dates, ¼ cup packed dark brown sugar, 4 tablespoons butter, and ⅓ cup heavy cream in a saucepan until the butter has melted. Scoop balls of vanilla ice cream into bowls, spoon the hot sauce over them, and top with some chopped toasted pecans.

2 **Roasted Dates with Rice Pudding**

Heat 24 pitted dates, 1 cup dry sherry, 2 tablesppons packed light brown sugar, 1 cinnamon stick, and a piece of orange rind in a saucepan until boiling. Pour into a small ovenproof dish and cook in a preheated oven, at 350°F, for 15 minutes, basting the dates a couple of times.

Discard the cinnamon stick and orange rind. Stir 1½ cups prepared rice pudding together with ⅔ cup lightly whipped heavy cream and place in serving dishes. Spoon the dates and sauce over the rice pudding before serving.

Summer Berry Charlotte

Serves 4

5 cups mixed berries, such as strawberries, raspberries, and blueberries

1 tablespoon flour

⅔ cup granulated sugar

1 teaspoon vanilla extract

4–6 slices of brioche bread

soft butter, for spreading

vanilla ice cream, to serve

- Toss together the berries, flour, sugar, and vanilla extract and place in an ovenproof dish.

- Cut the brioche slices into triangles, removing the crusts, if you like. Butter both sides of the brioche and arrange on top of the berries. Cover the dish with aluminum foil and then bake in a preheated oven, at 425°F, for 10 minutes. Uncover and cook for another 5 minutes, until golden and crisp. Serve with vanilla ice cream.

---

10 Berry Brioche Toasts

Heat 2 tablespoons butter in a skillet until melted. Add 2 cups fresh sliced strawberries and blueberries and ¼ cup granulated sugar. Swirl around the skillet until the sugar melts and the berries start to burst. Lightly toast 4 thick slices of brioche bread. Place on serving plates, spoon the berries with all the juices over the brioche, and serve with scoops of ice cream.

30 Simple Summer Pudding

Stir together ¼ cup black currant or blueberry syrup, 1 cup berry compote or preserves or your choice, and 4 cups mixed berries. Let sit for a couple of minutes, then drain, reserving the juices in a shallow bowl. Line a deep, round 5 cup ceramic bowl with plastic wrap. Cut out a circle from a slice of brioche to fit in the bottom of the bowl. Soak the brioche in the fruit juices, then place in the bowl. Cut another 6–8 slices of brioche into long strips, dip into the juices, and use to line the sides of the bowl, then spoon in the fruits to fill. Cover with some more brioche slices and pour over the remaining juices. Cover with plastic wrap, place a small plate on top, and weigh down with a heavy can. Let sit in the refrigerator for 10–15 minutes, then turn out onto a serving plate. Serve with cream.

30 Chocolate Peanut Butter Whoopie Pies

Serves 6–8

2⅓ cups all-purpose flour
⅔ cup unsweetened cocoa powder
2 teaspoons baking powder
2 teaspoons baking soda
⅔ cup firmly packed light brown sugar
1 egg, beaten
⅓ cup vegetable oil
⅔ cup buttermilk
⅓ cup boiling water
½ cup cream cheese
⅓ cup smooth peanut butter
1⅔ cups confectioners' sugar
4 oz semisweet chocolate

- Line a large baking sheet with parchment paper. Place the flour, cocoa, baking soda, and light brown sugar in a large bowl. Mix the egg, oil, and buttermilk with a boiling water and stir into the dry ingredients until well mixed. Spoon about 30 tablespoonfuls onto the baking sheet, making sure they are well spaced apart, and bake in a preheated oven, at 350°F, for 10–12 minutes or until just firm. Let cool.

- Beat together the cream cheese and peanut butter until smooth. Sift in the confectioners' sugar and beat until well combined. Pipe or spoon the filling over 15 halves, then sandwich the remaining 15 on top.

- Melt the chocolate over a small bowl set in a saucepan of simmering water, making sure the water does not touch the bottom of the bowl (or use a double boiler). Drizzle the melted chocolate over the whoopie pies before serving.

---

1 Chocolate Peanut Butter Shakes

For each shake, blend 2 scoops of vanilla ice cream with 1 cup milk, 3 tablespoons peanut butter, and ¼ cup prepared chocolate sauce until smooth. Pour into a large glass and top with some whipped cream and a coarsely chopped peanut chocolate bar.

2 Chocolate Peanut Butter Bites

Stamp out 12 circles from a sheet of store-bought rolled dough pie crust and use them to line a lightly greased 12-cup cupcake pan. Bake in a preheated oven, at 400°F, for 10 minutes or until golden. Press any puffed sides down with a teaspoon. Meanwhile, heat 2 tablespoons butter, ¼ cup heavy cream, 4 oz white chocolate, and 3 tablespoons peanut butter in a saucepan over low heat until smooth. Pour a little into each tart shell and place in the freezer to cool. Melt 2 oz semisweet chocolate in a bowl over a saucepan of simmering water and drizzle the melted chocolate over the bites to serve.

30 Individual Pear Crisps with an Oaty Topping

Serves 4

⅓ cup good-quality applesauce

4 Bosc pears, peeled, cored, and chopped

½ teaspoon ground cinnamon

¼ cup firmly packed light brown sugar

⅔ cup all-purpose flour

½ cup rolled oats

6 tablespoons butter

1 tablespoon light corn syrup

- Put the applesauce, pears, and cinnamon into a small saucepan and gently cook for 10 minutes, until softened. Spoon the mixture into 4 ramekins or ovenproof tea cups.

- Rub together the sugar, flour, oats, and butter to make a lumpy mixture. Stir in the light corn syrup. Sprinkle on top of the fruit and bake in a preheated oven, at 400°F, for 15 minutes, until golden and bubbling.

10 Pear and Oat Parfait

Finely chop 2 pears and simmer in ¼ cup water with 1 tablespoon lemon juice, a pinch of cinnamon, and 2 tablespoons light brown sugar for 5 minutes. Transfer to a metal bowl and cool in the freezer. Mix 1¼ cups Greek yogurt with 1 teaspoon vanilla extract and 2 tablespoons sugar. Place a spoonful of the pear sauce at the bottom of 4 serving dishes. Spoon some yogurt over the pear, then top with some crumbled store-bought oat bar. Repeat the layers, ending with crumbled oat bar and some toasted slivered almonds.

20 Baked Pear with Crumb Topping

Heat 2 tablespoons butter in a large skillet. Add 4 peeled, halved, and cored pears and cook for 5 minutes, then pour in ¼ cup orange juice and cook for another 2 minutes. Meanwhile, heat 4 tablespoons butter and 2 tablespoons honey in a saucepan, then stir in ½ cup oats. Put the pears on a baking sheet, cut side up, and sprinkle with the oat mixture. Bake in a preheated oven, at 400°F, for 5–10 minutes, until the topping is crunchy and the pears are soft. Serve with ice cream.

Banana Pecan Strudels

Serves 4

4 sheets of phyllo pastry
4 tablespoons butter, melted
¼ cup confectioners' sugar
¼ cup pecans, toasted and
  finely chopped
2 bananas, sliced lengthwise
  into quarters
½ cup mascarpone cheese
2 tablespoons maple syrup,
  plus extra for drizzling

- Unroll a pastry sheet, keeping the remainder covered with a damp but not wet cloth. Brush all over with some butter, then sift 1 tablespoon of the confectioners' sugar over the pastry and sprinkle with one-quarter of the pecans. Cut in half and place a banana quarter along both shorter ends. Fold in the long edges and roll up. Place on a baking sheet and repeat with the remaining pastry.

- Brush all over with more butter, then cook in a preheated oven, at 400°F, for 12–15 minutes, until crisp and golden.

- Mix the mascarpone with the maple syrup and serve alongside the pastries with more maple syrup drizzled over the top.

Warm Fudge and Banana Pecan

Splits Put 4 tablespoons butter, ½ cup firmly packed light brown sugar, and ½ cup heavy cream in a saucepan, bring to a boil, and simmer for 5 minutes. Cut 4 bananas in half and place in serving dishes. Top with scoops of vanilla ice cream, then drizzle the sauce over the top. Sprinkle with ¼ cup toasted pecans before serving.

Banana Pecan Crisp

Slice 4 bananas and mix with ⅓ cup each prepared caramel sauce and heavy cream. Place in an ovenproof dish. Blend together 1 cup all-purpose flour, ½ cup firmly packed light brown sugar, and 1 stick butter in a food processor until the mixture resembles bread crumbs. Stir in ½ cup rolled oats and ⅓ cup dry shredded coconut. Sprinkle with the bananas and cook in a preheated oven, at 350°F, for 25 minutes or until golden and bubbling.

Lemon Puddings

Serves 4

4 tablespoons butter
⅔ cup granulated sugar
2 eggs, separated
⅓ cup all-purpose flour
⅔ cup milk
⅔ cup light cream
finely grated rind of 1 lemon and
    juice of ½ lemon
confectioners' sugar, to serve

- Put the butter and sugar in a bowl and beat with a handheld electric mixer until pale and creamy. Add the egg yolks and mix in well, then stir in the flour. Gradually whisk in the milk and cream, followed by the lemon rind and juice.

- Whisk the egg whites until stiff peaks form. Stir one-third of the whites into the batter. Then carefully fold in the remainder, half at a time. Spoon the batter into 4 individual ramekins and bake in a preheated oven, at 350°F, for 15 minutes or until golden. Dust with confectioners' sugar to serve.

 Lemon Baskets
Mix together 1 cup crème fraîche or sour cream and ½ cup lemon curd until smooth. Spoon into 4 prepared brandy snap baskets. Sprinkle a handful of blackberries on top, dust with confectioners' sugar, and serve.

 Lemon Mousse
Using a handheld electric mixer, mix together 1¼ cups heavy cream, ⅓ cup granulated sugar, and the finely grated rind of 1 lemon. Stir in 1 tablespoon lemon juice or to taste and mix until smooth.

Whisk 2 egg whites until stiff peaks form. Stir a spoonful of the mixture into the whipped cream, then carefully fold in the remainder, half at a time. Spoon into serving bowls and grate some more lemon rind over the top to serve.

Seared Pineapple with Rum and Coconut

Serves 6

2 tablespoons butter
¼ cup firmly packed brown sugar
1 pineapple, peeled and
   cut into wedges
2 tablespoons rum
⅓ cup dry shredded coconut
coconut or vanilla ice cream,
   to serve

- Heat the butter in a large skillet until melted. Sprinkle half the sugar over the pineapple and cook for 3 minutes, until caramelized. Turn the wedges over and cook for another 2 minutes. Remove the pineapple from the skillet.

- Take the skillet off the heat and add the rum and remaining sugar. Return to the heat and simmer until thickened.

- Meanwhile, place the coconut in a small, dry skillet and cook for 1–2 minutes, stirring frequently, until lightly browned. Put the pineapple slices on serving plates with scoops of ice cream. Drizzle with the sauce and sprinkle with the coconut to serve.

---

2 Pineapple Pancakes with Coconut Sauce Mix 1⅔ cups all-purpose flour with 2 teaspoons baking powder and a pinch of salt. Beat in 1 egg and 1¼ cups milk. Heat a little butter in a nonstick skillet. Add 3 tablespoonfuls of batter. Place a pineapple slice on top of each and cook for 2–3 minutes on each side, until puffed and golden. Keep warm and repeat with the remaining batter. Meanwhile, mix ¼ cup granulated sugar with a little water, heat for 2 minutes, until melted, and cook until dark gold. Remove from heat and stir in ⅔ cup coconut milk. Heat through and spoon over the pancakes.

3 Individual Pineapple and Coconut Cakes Grease 6 large ramekins and coat with 1 tablespoon granulated sugar, shaking away any excess. Place 1 canned pineapple slice in the bottom of each ramekin. In a food processor, blend together 1¼ sticks softened butter, ¾ cup granulated sugar, 1¼ cups all-purpose flour, and 1 teaspoon baking powder with 2 eggs and ⅓ cup dry shredded coconut until smooth. Spoon the batter into the ramekins and bake in a preheated oven, at 350°F, for 20–25 minutes, until just cooked through. Meanwhile, melt 4 tablespoons butter and ¼ cup firmly packed light brown sugar in a saucepan. Cook for 2–3 minutes, then take off the heat and carefully pour in 2 tablespoons rum. Turn out the cakes onto plates and spoon the sauce over them.

 # Raspberry Tiramisu

Serves 4

2 egg yolks
¼ cup granulated sugar
¼ cup Marsala wine
1¼ cups heavy cream
1 cup mascarpone cheese
½ cup strong coffee, cooled
16 ladyfingers
2 oz semisweet chocolate, grated
1⅔ cups raspberries

- Put the egg yolks and 2 tablespoons each sugar and Marsala into a small bowl set over a saucepan of simmering water, making sure the bottom of the bowl does not touch the water (or use a double boiler). Whisk the mixture until fluffy and it holds a trail when the whisk is lifted out of the bowl. Keep whisking until cooled.

- Whisk the cream until soft peaks form. Beat together the mascarpone and the remaining sugar and stir this into the cooled egg mixture, followed by the whipped cream.

- Put the coffee and remaining Marsala into a shallow bowl. Dip some of the ladyfingers in the mixture and place in the bottom of 4 serving bowls. Sprinkle with some chocolate and raspberries, then spoon some of the cream mixture over the top. Repeat the layers until the mixture is used up. Top with grated chocolate to serve.

---

1 ### Crunchy Raspberry and Meringue

Desserts Lightly crush 3 small meringues. Mix together ¾ cup mascarpone cheese with ⅔ cup store-bought vanilla pudding. Stir with the crushed meringue and 1¼ cups raspberries. Place in serving bowls and grate some semisweet chocolate over the top before serving.

3 ### Raspberry Mascarpone Puffs

Cut out 4 circles, each 2 inches across, from a sheet of ready-to-bake puff pastry. Place on a lightly greased baking sheet and brush all over with egg yolk. Cook in a preheated oven, at 400°F, for 10–15 minutes, until golden and crisp. Let cool. Mix together 1 cup mascarpone cheese, 2–3 tablespoons granulated sugar, and 1 teaspoon vanilla extract. Spoon the mixture over the cooled pastry. Sprinkle with a handful of raspberries and some chocolate curls to serve.

White Chocolate Rice Pudding Brûlée

Serves 4

⅔ cup short-grain rice
1 cup milk
1¼ cups light cream
½ cup granulated sugar
1 teaspoon vanilla extract
2 egg yolks
3 oz white chocolate, chopped

- Cook the rice in a large saucepan of boiling water for 5 minutes and drain well. Return to the pan and pour in the milk, cream, ¼ cup of the sugar, and the vanilla extract. Cook over medium heat for 15–20 minutes, until soft and creamy. Remove from the heat and stir through the egg yolks and white chocolate until smooth.

- Spoon the mixture into 4 individual heatproof ramekins and smooth over the top with the spoon. Let cool a little, then sprinkle with the remaining granulated sugar. Place under a preheated hot broiler and cook for 1 minute, until the sugar caramelizes. Let cool until the surface is hard, then serve.

10 White Chocolate Crispy Rice Squares

Melt 4 tablespoons butter and 4 oz white chocolate in a saucepan. Add 1 (10 oz) package marshmallows and stir until melted, then add 7 cups crispy rice cereal and stir until well coated. Line an 8 × 12 inch baking pan with parchment paper and pour in the mixture. Let cool, then cut into squares and pile onto plates to serve.

20 Chocolate Custard and Rice Tarts

Melt 3 oz white chocolate in a bowl over a saucepan of gently simmering water and let cool a little (or use a double boiler). Mix 1 cup cooked rice pudding and 1¼ cups store-bought vanilla pudding with 1 egg yolk. Stir in the chocolate and 2 tablespoons raisins. Spoon into 4 prepared tart shells and bake in a preheated oven, at 350°F, for 12–15 minutes, until the filling is just set. Dust with a little ground cinnamon to serve.

Apple, Maple, and Pecan Whips

Serves 4

¾ cup good-quality applesauce
1 Granny Smith apple, peeled and grated or finely chopped
1 cup heavy cream
1 cup store-bought vanilla pudding
3 tablespoons maple syrup
¼ cup pecans, toasted and chopped
pecan cookies, to serve

- Put the applesauce and apple in a small saucepan, cook for 5 minutes to soften, then place in metal bowl in the freezer for a few minutes to cool.

- Whip the cream until soft peaks form, then stir in the pdding. Swirl through the applesauce and maple syrup, then spoon into serving dishes. Top with toasted pecans and serve with pecan cookies.

2 Apple and Pecan Brioches

Core and thinly slice 2 Braeburn apples, arrange on a baking sheet, and brush over a little melted butter. Cook under a preheated medium broiler for 3 minutes on each side, until lightly golden. Mix ⅔ cup each of milk and cream with 1 egg and 1 teaspoon vanilla extract. Dip 8 slices of brioche in the milk mixture until well coated. Heat a little butter in a nonstick skillet and cook the brioche, in batches, for 2–3 minutes on each side, until golden. Arrange the apple slices on top, add spoonfuls of crème fraîche or whipped cream, and sprinkle with chopped pecans. Drizzle with a little maple syrup to serve.

3 Apple and Pecan Tart

Unwrap a sheet of ready-to-bake puff pastry onto a lightly greased baking sheet. Score around the edge with a sharp knife, being careful not to cut right through the pastry, to make a ½ inch border. Brush 1 beaten egg over this border. Core and slice 6 Granny Smith apples. Toss with 1 teaspoon ground cinnamon and 2 tablespoons granulated sugar and sprinkle the apples over the tart. Cook in a preheated oven, at 400°F, for 20 minutes, then sprinkle with ¼ cup chopped pecans and cook for another 2 minutes, until crisp and lightly golden. Drizzle with 2 tablespoons maple syrup and serve.

 # Strawberry Rhubarb Shortcake Slices

Serves 4–6

1 stick cold butter, cubed,
  plus extra for greasing
2⅓ cups all-purpose flour
1 tablespoon baking powder
3 tablespoons granulated sugar
1 egg, beaten
⅔ cup milk
¾ cup sliced rhubarb
¼ cup firmly packed light
  brown sugar
finely grated rind of 1 orange
½ cup port
1¼ cups heavy cream
1 cup small or halved
  hulled strawberries

- Lightly grease a baking sheet. Put the butter, flour, baking powder, and 2 tablespoons granulated sugar in a large bowl or food processor. Rub or blend together until the mixture resembles coarse bread crumbs. Mix together the egg and milk and pour into the bowl. Cut through the mixture with a fork until it is just combined. Roll out the dough on a lightly floured surface until it is about 4 × 8 inches, trimming the edges. Place on the baking sheet and bake in a preheated oven, at 350°F, for 15–20 minutes, until golden. Let cool.

- Meanwhile, put the rhubarb, brown sugar, orange rind, and port in a saucepan with a splash of water, cover, and cook for 5 minutes, then cook for another 5 minutes, uncovered, until the rhubarb is soft. Place in a metal bowl in the freezer and let cool.

- Whip the cream and the remaining granulated sugar until soft peaks form. Place the shortcake on a serving dish. Swirl the whipped cream over the shortcake, spoon the rhubarb compote over the cream, and arrange the strawberries on top. Cut into slices to serve.

Rhubarb Strawberry Dunkers Blend together 1 cup hulled strawberries in a food processor with ½ cup canned rhubarb and sugar to taste until a smooth sauce forms. Stir through ¾ cup ricotta and divide among 6 serving bowls. Drizzle with 1 tablespoon honey and serve with shortbread cookies for dunking.

Strawberry and Rhubarb Tarts Cut a sheet of ready-to-bake puff pastry into 6 rectangles. Mix together 3 tablespoons crème fraîche or heavy cream with ¼ cup granulated sugar and spread over the center of each rectangle. Top with ⅔ cup sliced rhubarb and ¾ cup halved strawberries. Sift 3 tablespoons confectioners' sugar over the top and bake in a preheated oven, at 425°F, for 15 minutes, until golden.

Caramelized Custard Tarts

Serves 4

1 sheet ready-to-bake
  puff pastry
pinch of ground nutmeg
½ teaspoon ground cinnamon
2 tablespoons granulated sugar

Filling

3 egg yolks
¼ cup granulated sugar
2 tablespoons cornstarch
1 teaspoon vanilla extract
finely grated rind of ¼ lemon
1¼ cups heavy cream

- Unwrap the pastry and sprinkle with the nutmeg, cinnamon, and 2 tablespoons granulated sugar. Then tightly roll up the pastry, like a jelly roll, and cut it into twelve ¾ inch slices (you may have some pastry left over). Roll each slice into a small circle on a lightly floured surface. Turn a 12-cup muffin pan upside down, gently press each circle over the bottom of a muffin cup, and chill in the freezer for 5 minutes.

- Bake in a preheated oven, at 425°F, for 5 minutes, then place the pastry shells on a baking sheet.

- Meanwhile, for the filling, put the egg yolks, the granulated sugar, cornstarch, vanilla extract, and lemon rind in a bowl and whisk until smooth. Add the cream and whisk again, then cook in a saucepan for 5 minutes, stirring frequently, until the mixture is thick, being careful not to let it boil. Spoon the custard into the pastry shells. Turn up the oven to 450°F, and bake for 12–15 minutes, until caramelized and set.

1 Creamy Caramel

Whip 1¼ cups heavy cream until soft peaks form, then stir in 3 tablespoons prepared caramel sauce. Spoon into 4 serving bowls. Sprinkle with a little ground cinnamon and drizzle with some more caramel sauce. Serve with tuile cookies.

2 Caramel and Banana Tart

In a food processor, blend 10 oz oatmeal cookies until small crumbs form, then pulse in 6 tablespoons butter, melted. Press into a 9 inch tart pan and cook in a preheated oven, at 350°F, for 10–12 minutes, until golden and crisp. Let cool a little, then spread ⅓ cup store-bought dulce de leche (caramel sauce) on top. Slice 2 bananas and place on top of the sauce. Whip 1¼ cups heavy cream with 1 tablespoon granulated sugar. Spoon the cream over the bananas and top with a little grated chocolate.

Warm Chocolate Cherry Tarts

Serves 4

8 oz semisweet chocolate,
  broken into pieces
3 tablespoons heavy cream
1 tablespoon brandy
2 eggs and 1 egg yolk
¼ cup granulated sugar
¼ cup halved natural
  candied cherries
4 prepared individual pastry shells

- Put the chocolate, cream, and brandy in a small bowl. Set it over a saucepan of gently simmering water, so the bottom of the bowl is not touching the water, and heat for a couple of minutes, until the chocolate is melted (or use a double boiler). Let cool a little.

- Whisk together the eggs, egg yolk, and sugar with a handheld electric mixer until pale and creamy. Carefully stir the chocolate mixture into the eggs. Arrange the cherries in the pastry shells, pour the chocolate mixture over the cherries, and bake in a preheated oven, at 375°F, for 12 minutes or until just set.

10 Cherries with Chocolate Dipping

Sauce Heat 1 cup heavy cream in a saucepan until boiling. Put 8 oz chopped semisweet chocolate in a bowl. Pour the cream over the chocolate and stir until smooth. Add a splash of brandy or kirsch, if liked. Place in a warm serving bowl and serve with fresh cherries for dunking.

30 Individual Chocolate Cherry

Cakes Put 1¼ sticks softened butter, ⅔ cup granulated sugar, 1 cup all-purpose flour, ¼ cup cocoa powder, 2 teaspoons baking powder, 3 eggs, and 3 tablespoons milk in a food processor and blend until smooth. Butter and flour 4 ramekins and spoon the batter into them. Bake in a preheated oven, at 350°F, for 12–15 minutes, until just cooked through. Turn the cakes out and let cool. Meanwhile, whip 1 cup heavy cream with 2 tablespoons confectioners' sugar. Pit 1 cup fresh cherries. Cut each cake in half horizontally. Spread a little cream over the bottom halves and add 1 teaspoon cherry preserves to each. Top with the other halves, then spoon more cream on top and finish with fresh cherries.

 # Passion Fruit Cheesecakes

Serves 6

1¼ cups crushed gingersnap cookies

4 tablespoons butter, melted, plus extra for greasing

1¾ cups cream cheese

⅔ cup confectioners' sugar, sifted

2 teaspoons vanilla extract

1 cup heavy cream

3 passion fruits

- Mix together the crushed gingersnaps and butter. Place 6 metal rings, each 3½ inches across, on serving plates. Alternatively, cut 12 strips of parchment paper and place 2 in a cross shape in the bottom of 6 lightly greased individual ramekins, leaving the ends hanging over the sides. Press the crumbs into the bottom of the rings or ramekins and put them in the freezer while you make the filling.

- Beat together the cream cheese, confectioners' sugar, and vanilla extract until smooth. Then beat in the heavy cream until the mixture thickens. Spoon the mixture into the rings or ramekins and return to the freezer for about 10 minutes, until firmly set.

- Carefully ease the rings off the cheesecakes or lift them from the ramekins, using the parchment paper. Scoop out the passion fruit pulp and spoon it over the cheesecakes to serve.

1 **Bananas in Passion Fruit and Ginger Syrup** Put ⅔ cup passion fruit pulp in a small saucepan with a knob of peeled fresh root ginger, ½ cup each sweet dessert wine and water, and ⅓ cup granulated sugar and boil for 5 minutes, until syrupy. Remove the ginger. Halve 6 bananas and place them in serving bowls. Spoon the warm syrup over the bananas and serve with yogurt.

2 **Passion Fruit Curd Desserts** Place ⅔ cup passion fruit pulp in a pan along with 1½ sticks butter, 1 cup granulated sugar, and 1 tablespoon lemon juice and warm to melt the butter. Whisk together 3 eggs and 2 egg yolks. Add 2 tablespoons of the passion fruit pulp and stir together, then pour all the mixture back into the pan. Cook over low heat for 3–5 minutes or until the mixture has thickened. Pour into a bowl and chill in the refrigerator. Put 1 cup lightly crushed gingersnap cookies in the bottom of 6 serving glasses. Whisk 1 cup heavy cream until soft peaks form and stir together with 2 tablespoons confectioners' sugar and 1 cup mascarpone cheese. Layer the cream mixture in the glasses with the passion fruit curd, topping with some fresh passion fruit pulp.

1 Warm Mango and Raspberry Gratin

Serves 4

½ cup heavy cream
⅔ cup mascarpone cheese
1 cup prepared pastry cream
  or whipped cream
1 mango, peeled, pitted and sliced
2 cups raspberries

- Whip the cream until soft peaks form, then carefully stir together with the mascarpone and pastry cream.

- Put the mango and raspberries in a small, shallow ovenproof dish and spread the cream mixture on top. Cook in a hot broiler for 2–3 minutes, until lightly browned.

2 Mango and Raspberry Pastry

Stacks Cut 1 sheet ready-to-bake puff pastry into 12 rectangles and place on a baking sheet. Cover with another baking sheet and cook in a preheated oven, at 400°F, for 10 minutes or until golden and crisp. Uncover and sift 2 tablespoons confectioners' sugar over them. Place under a hot broiler for 30 seconds, until the sugar melts, then let cool. Mix together ⅔ cup heavy cream, whipped to soft peaks, with ¾ cup mascarpone cheese, 3 tablespoons confectioners' sugar, and 1 teaspoon vanilla extract. Place 4 pastry pieces on serving plates. Spoon over some cream and arrange mango slices and raspberries on top. Repeat the layers, finishing with a piece of pastry.

3 Mango Cakes with Raspberry Sauce

Butter 4 individual ramekins or dariole molds. Mix together 2 tablespoons each softened butter and brown sugar and spoon the mixture into the bottom of the ramekins. Add 1 tablespoon chopped mango to each ramekin. Blend together 1 stick softened butter, ½ cup granulated sugar, ¾ cup all-purpose flour, and ¾ cup baking powder with 2 eggs and 1 teaspoon vanilla extract until a smooth batter forms. Spoon the batter into the ramekins and cook in a preheated oven, at 350°F, for 20–25 minutes, until just cooked through. Press 1¼ cups raspberries through a strainer and sift in 1 tablespoon confectioners' sugar to make a sauce. Spoon the sauce over the cakes to serve.

 # Orange and Cinnamon Puddings with Syrup

Serves 4

1 stick butter, softened, plus
  extra for greasing
¼ cup light corn syrup, plus extra
  for serving
2 large oranges
½ cup firmly packed light
  brown sugar
1¼ cups all-purpose flour
1 teaspoon baking powder
½ teaspoon ground cinnamon
2 eggs

- Grease 4 individual dessert molds or ramekins and divide the light corn syrup among them. Finely grate the rind of both oranges and place in a food processor, then use a sharp knife to remove the pith. Thickly slice 1 orange. Carefully arrange 1 orange slice at the bottom of each mold. Chop the remaining orange flesh, removing any pith or seeds, and place in the food processor together with the remaining ingredients. Blend to make a smooth batter.

- Spoon the batter into the molds. Place in a roasting pan filled halfway with boiling water. Cover with aluminum foil and bake in a preheated oven, at 350°F, for 20–25 minutes, until just cooked through. Let sit for a minute in the molds, then turn out onto plates and serve with a little more light corn syrup drizzled over, if liked.

1 Caramel Oranges with Cinnamon

Yogurt Heat ⅓ cup firmly packed light brown sugar in a large skillet with ⅓ cup heavy cream and 2 tablespoons butter until the butter has melted. Peel and thickly slice 6 oranges and add to the skillet. Swirl the sauce over the oranges and cook for another 2 minutes. Spoon out onto plates. Mix ⅔ cup plain yogurt together with 1 teaspoon cinnamon and spoon it over the oranges before serving.

2 Orange and Cinnamon Tart

Unwrap a sheet of store-bought rolled dough pie crust onto a lightly greased baking sheet, crimp around the edges, and bake in a preheated oven, at 400°F, for 12 minutes or until golden and crisp. Let cool. Stir 1 cup cream cheese with the finely grated rind and juice of 1 orange, 1 teaspoon cinnamon, and 2 tablespoons confectioners' sugar. Spoon the cream cheese mixture over the pastry. Peel and slice 2 oranges and arrange the slices on top.

Honey Ricotta Fritters with Pistachios

Serves 4

¾ cup ricotta
1 egg, lightly beaten
⅓ cup all-purpose flour
2 tablespoons granulated sugar
finely grated rind and juice of
 1 orange
oil, for frying
⅓ cup honey
3 tablespoons chopped pistachios
salt
Greek yogurt, to serve (optional)

- Drain any water from the ricotta, then mix the cheese with the egg until smooth. Stir in the flour, sugar, and orange rind together with a pinch of salt.

- Fill a large saucepan one-third full of oil and heat it until a small piece of bread dropped in the oil sizzles and turns brown after 15 seconds. Drop spoonfuls of the ricotta mixture into the oil and cook for 1–2 minutes, until golden and puffed. Let drain on paper towels.

- Meanwhile, heat the orange juice and honey in a small saucepan until well combined. Place the warm fritters on serving plates and drizzle with the honey syrup. Sprinkle the chopped pistachios over the top and serve with yogurt, if liked.

---

1 **Fresh Fruit with Honey Ricotta Dip**

Stir together ¾ cup ricotta, 1 tablespoon honey, and 1 teaspoon vanilla extract. Place in a serving bowl, sprinkle with some chopped pistachios, and serve with strawberries and melon slices for dipping.

3 **Ricotta Puddings with Honey Syrup**

Whisk 2 egg whites until stiff peaks form. Drain any water from 1 cup ricotta and beat together with 2 tablespoons granulated sugar and 1 teaspoon vanilla extract until smooth. Stir in a large spoonful of the egg white, then carefully fold in the remaining egg white, half at a time. Lightly grease 4 individual ramekins. Spoon the ricotta mixture into them and bake in a preheated oven, at 325°F, for 20 minutes or until a toothpick inserted into the center of a pudding comes out clean. Let sit for a minute, then turn out onto plates. Drizzle with ¼ cup honey and sprinkle with some chopped pistachios.

Index

Italic pagination indicates photographs